knit 1, purl 2
in Crochet

Contents

Introduction

In knitting, there are two basic stitches, the knit stitch and the purl stitch. Although long thought to be unique to knitters, these versatile little stitches are available to crocheters as well. Using one stick, with a hook on the end, crocheters can now Knit 1 and Purl 2.

To work a knit stitch: One places the yarn in the back of the work, then inserts the crochet hook or the knitting needle through the stitch (one loop only) from the front of the work to the back of the work, yarn is wrapped around the crochet hook or the knitting needle, then pulled through the stitch.

To work a purl stitch: One places the yarn in the front of the work, then inserts the crochet hook or the knitting needle through a stitch (one loop only) from the back of the work to the front of the work, yarn is wrapped around the crochet hook or the knitting needle, then pulled through the stitch.

Using a crochet hook, instead of a knitting needle, creates only one extra step. When using a crochet hook, the wrapped yarn that is pulled through the stitch must also be pulled through the loop on the hook. In knitting, this is known as binding off.

By combining knit and purl stitches within a given work, one can crochet beautiful fabric including cables, ribbing, bobbles and a variety of texture stitches.

BASIC INSTRUCTIONS

As a guide, to translate knitting instructions and abbreviations into crochet instructions, one can use the following chart. Keep in mind that the chart is only a guide and when following the chart not all finished crocheted fabric will look like its knitted counterpart.

KNIT ABBREVIATIONS	CROCHET INSTRUCTIONS
Knit (K)	Yarn in back, insert hook from front to back through 1 lp of st, yo, pull through st and lp on hook.
Purl (P)	Yarn in front, insert hook from back to front through 1 lp of st, yo, pull through st and lp on hook.
Yarn in back (yib)	Place yarn in back of work.
Yarn in front (yif)	Place yarn in front of work.
Bind off (BO)	Pull 2nd lp on hook over first lp (first lp is the lp closest to the head of the hook).
Knit-wise	Insert hook in st as if to knit.
Purl-wise	Insert hook in st as if to purl.
Slip, slip, knit (ssk)	Insert hook knit wise in each of next 2 sts, yo, pull through both sts and lp on hook. St slants to the left.
Slip 1, knit 1 (psso)	Work same as ssk.
Slip 1	Insert hook in next st.
Yarn over (yo)	Yarn over then bind off (work ch 1).
Knit 2 together (K2tog)	Sk next st, insert hook knit wise through next st then insert hook knit wise through sk st, yo, pull through both sts and lp on hook. St slants to right.
Slip, Slip, purl (ssp)	Worked on WS rows, sk next st, insert hook purl wise through next st then insert hook purl wise through sk st, yo, pull through both sts and lp on hook. St slants to left on RS facing.

KNIT ABBREVIATIONS	CROCHET INSTRUCTIONS
Purl 2 together (P2tog)	Worked on WS rows, insert hook purl wise in each of next 2 sts, yo, pull through both sts and lp on hook. St slants to right on RS facing.
Make 1 knit left (M1K-L)	Insert hook knit wise through same st where last st was made, then insert hook knit wise through next st, yo, pull through both sts and lp on hook.
Make 1 knit right (M1K-R)	Insert hook knit wise through next st, then insert hook knit wise through previous st, yo, pull through both sts and lp on hook.
Make 1 purl left (M1P-L)	Worked on WS rows, insert hook purl wise through next st, then insert hook purl wise through previous st, yo, pull through both sts and lp on hook. St slants to left on RS facing.
Make 1 purl right (M1P-R)	Worked on WS rows, insert hook purl wise through same st where last st was made, then insert hook purl wise through next st, yo, pull through both sts and lp on hook. St slants to right on RS facing.
Selvage	On RS rows knit the front lp of the first and last st on the row. On WS rows knit the back lp of the first and last st on the row.

YARNS & HOOKS

TYPES OF YARN TO USE

Yarns that have fiber memory work well when knitting and purling with a crochet hook. When first learning the technique, smooth, light-colored, acrylic yarns are recommended. Wool yarn and yarn blends are also good choices. Due to the nature of the yarn, cotton is not recommended.

HOOK SIZE TO USE

When working crocheted knit and purl stitches, one should use a hook larger than the hook size recommended on the yarn label.

As a general rule of thumb, unless one desires a tight stitch for a purse or other similar item, the following hook sizes are recommended:

For sport weight yarn (# 3 light) – use size US K/10.5/6.5mm or larger hook.

For worsted weight yarn (#4 medium) – use size US L/11/8mm or larger hook.

HOOK TIP

When working stitches, one can insert the hook through the stitch by pushing the point of the hook through the stitch or by catching the loop of the stitch with the lip of hook.

Stitch swatches in this book were crocheted using (#4 medium) worsted weight yarn with a Susan Bates® Luxite® (8mm) L-11 and a Susan Bates® Luxite® (9mm) M-13 crochet hook.

TENSION

Crochet is no place to have tension. Leave the stress of the day behind. When knitting and purling with a crochet hook, relax and keep stitches loose.

CASTING ON & BINDING OFF

CAST ON/BIND OFF (CO/BO)

This creates the beginning row of every project. Determine where to make the beginning slip knot (see: How to estimate where to make the beginning slip knot). Make a slip knot (see How to make a slip knot). Cast on (CO) 1 stitch (see: How to work a slingshot cast-on). Bind off (BO) the beginning slip knot (see: How to bind off). *CO another stitch then BO the previous stitch, rep from * till the required number of stitches has been worked.

CASTING ON/BINDING OFF TIP

The cast on/bind off row needs to be as loose as the rest of the fabric one is crocheting; if need be, use a hook a size or two larger for the cast on/bind off row.

HOW TO ESTIMATE WHERE TO MAKE THE BEGINNING SLIP KNOT

Allow 10 inches plus approximately 1 inch for each stitch to be cast on. For instance, if one needs 5 beginning stitches, one would add 10 inches plus 5 inches for a total of 15 inches. The slip knot, for a beginning stitch count of 5, should be made approximately 15 inches from the end.

HOW TO MAKE A SLIP KNOT

Hold tail end of yarn in right hand, wrap yarn all the way around thumb and forefinger of left hand, drop yarn from right hand, spread left thumb and left forefinger open, then reach right thumb and forefinger through opening, grab yarn tail with right hand and pull through opening (do not pull tail end all the way through). Pull strands to tighten slip knot.

HOW TO WORK A SLINGSHOT CAST ON (CO)

Holding hook in right hand, place slip knot on hook so that the yarn tail is in front of hook and yarn is in back of hook. Place left thumb and left forefinger between the strands, hold the strands with the remaining left-hand fingers, spread left thumb and left forefinger open (*see Photo A*).

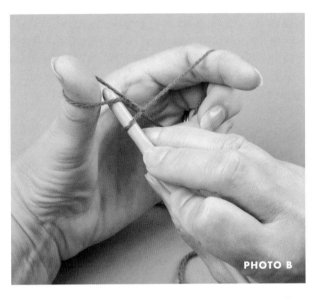

PHOTO B

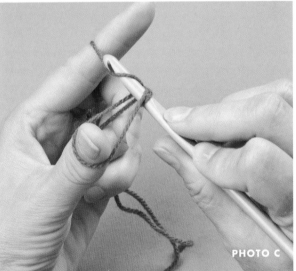

PHOTO C

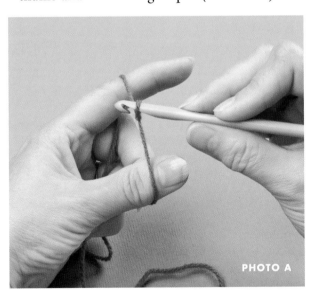

PHOTO A

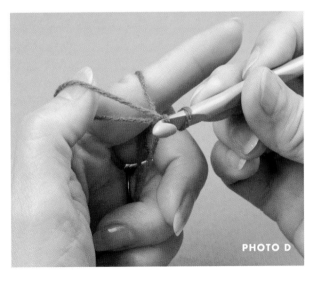

PHOTO D

Going front to back, place hook under strand in front of thumb going through loop on thumb (*see Photo B*), yarn over with yarn strand in front of finger (*see Photo C*), pull through loop on thumb (*see Photo D*), drop loop on thumb. Insert thumb between strands to tighten loop on hook.

HOW TO BIND OFF (BO)

Remove slip knot or previous loop from hook by pulling it over loop just made and off the hook (*See photos E–G*).

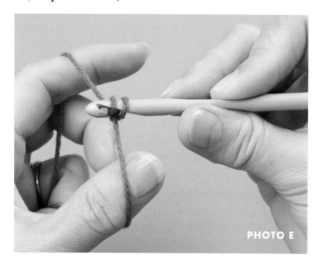

PHOTO E

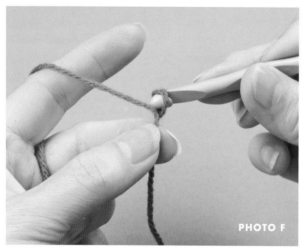

PHOTO F

PHOTO G

STITCH GUIDE

Knit: Place yarn in back of work, with hook facing down, insert hook from front to back through indicated stitch, yarn over, pull through stitch and loop on hook.

Twisted Knit: Place yarn in back of work, with hook facing down, insert hook from front to back through indicated stitch, yarn over, pull through stitch and loop on hook. Turn hook completely around counterclockwise, twisting loop on hook.

Purl: Place yarn in front of work, insert hook from back to front through indicated stitch, yarn over and pull through stitch and loop on hook.

Twisted Purl: Place yarn in front of work, insert hook from back to front through indicated stitch, yarn over and pull through stitch and loop on hook, turn hook completely around counterclockwise, twisting loop on hook.

READING INSTRUCTIONS

INSTRUCTIONS STATE:

1. Which stitch to use, knit or purl.
2. How many times to use the stitch.
3. Which loop the stitch is to be worked in.

EXAMPLES:

Knit 6 in front lps: Means knit in the **front loop** (*see Stitch Guide*) of each of the next 6 stitches.

Purl 2 in back lps: Means purl in the **back loop** (*see Stitch Guide*) of each of the next 2 stitches.

When knit terms are used in directions, such as slip 1, knit 1, psso, instructions for how to do the stitch in crochet are placed in Special Stitches at beginning of pattern.

CABLES

Cable directions are written in the following order:

A number followed by Front (F) or Back (B): Indicates how many stitches to place on the cable needle and whether to hold them in the front or in the back of the work.

Knit or Purl followed by a number: Indicates how to work the next stitches on the row knit (K) or purl (P) and how many to work.

K or P followed by C: Indicates how to work the stitches, Knit (K) or Purl (P), on the Cable (C) needle.

EXAMPLE:

1B/K3/PC means place 1 stitch on the cable needle or 2nd crochet hook and hold in back of the work (1B), knit each of the next 3 stitches on the row (K3), purl all of the stitches on the cable needle or 2nd crochet hook (PC).

ONE LOOP OR TWO

When knitting, one inserts the knitting needle under one loop to make a knit and or a purl stitch. The same is true when making knit and or purl stitches with a crochet hook.

Crocheted knit and purl stitches are made by inserting the hook under either the front loop or back loop of the stitch.

TO SKIP OR NOT TO SKIP

When knitting, the stitches to be worked are kept on a knitting needle. If one were to drop a stitch, the fabric would have a run in it. Because of this, stitches are generally not skipped (left unworked).

When working knit and purl stitches with a crochet hook, although the crocheted stitches would not unravel if skipped, one follows the same no-skipping-stitches rule.

CHAINS & TURNS

TURNING CHAINS

There are no turning chains at the beginning of crocheted knit and purl rows.

TURNING DIRECTION

Rows can be turned in any direction one prefers, as long as the method is consistent throughout the work. After turning the row, the yarn strand needs to be placed between the hook and the first stitch so that the first stitch is actually being worked over the yarn strand.

After turning the work, if the yarn is in back and needs to be in front, or if the yarn is in front and needs to be in back, move the strand between the left side of the hook and the fabric so that it is in the correct location. The first stitch of the new row will be worked over the yarn strand.

After turning the work, if the yarn is in the back and needs to be in the back or if the yarn is in the front and needs to be in the front, move the yarn strand to the right of the hook around the outer side of the fabric then to the left of the hook crossing the fabric so that the yarn strand is back to its original location. This will place the yarn strand between the hook and the first stitch so that the first stitch of the new row will be worked over the yarn strand.

TURNING WITHOUT CHAINING TIP

If one is having trouble seeing the first or the last stitch on a row due to the lack of a chain-1, try placing a marker in the stitch to help with location until the technique becomes more familiar.

BLOCKING

Some knitted items have a natural tendency to curl. When working knit and purl stitches with a crochet hook, one sees this same phenomena. To make the fabric lie flat, one can block the finished piece.

To block work so that it will lie flat, using no-rust pins, pin the fabric in the desired size and shape to a cushioned board. A quilter's cut and press board works well for this purpose due to the ruled lines, showing inches and various other measurements, which are preprinted on the padded board.

Steam the piece by placing an iron one or two inches above the work and pressing the steam button. One might need to press the steam button several times depending on the iron being used. Never allow the iron to touch the crocheted fabric itself. Once the fabric is steamed, leave the fabric pinned to the board until it is cool and completely dry.

ROW TERMINOLOGY

Current row: The row one is working on.
Previous row or 1 row below: The row one is working the current rows stitches into.
2 rows below: The row below the previous row.

EXAMPLE:

If one is following the directions for row 6:
Row 6 would be the current row.
Row 5 would be the previous row.
Row 4 would be the row 2 rows below.

KNIT 1, PURL 2 IN CROCHET

All of the designs in this book are created using two stitches, the Knit Stitch and the Purl Stitch. Although the stitches are worked with a crochet hook, they are worked in a similar fashion as if using knitting needles.

Just as in knitting, crocheted knit stitches and crocheted purl stitches can be worked through the front loop of a stitch or through the back loop of a stitch. In addition, crocheted knit stitches and crocheted purl stitches can be twisted counterclockwise. This creates eight variations; however, since the knit and purl stitches become mirror images of each other, this breaks down to four.

Mirror image means that they look the same except that the knit stitches lie horizontally from right to left and the purl stitches lie horizontally from left to right.

When working the same stitch for every row, the difference is barely noticeable in the finished fabric. However, as will be seen later in the book, by using each stitch's unique feature, one can create numerous stitch combinations. ∎

Mirror, Mirror Knit & Purl

Swatch #1

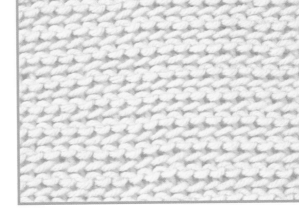

Knit front loop is a mirror image of purl back loop. Work either set of instructions to create Swatch #1.

SPECIAL STITCHES
Cast On/Bind Off (CO/BO): See instructions and photos in Introduction on pages 6–8.
Knit: With yarn in back, insert hook from front to back in lp indicated, yo, pull through st and lp on hook.
Purl: With yarn in front, insert hook from back to front in lp indicated, yo, pull through st and lp on hook.

INSTRUCTIONS

KNIT FRONT LOOP
Row 1: CO/BO (see Special Stitches) any number of sts, turn.
Row 2: Knit (see Special Stitches) in **front lps** (see Stitch Guide) across, turn.
Rep row 2 for pattern.

PURL BACK LOOP
Row 1: CO/BO (see Special Stitches) any number of sts, turn.
Row 2: Purl (see Special Stitches) in **back lps** (see Stitch Guide) across, turn.
Rep row 2 for pattern. ■

Swatch #2

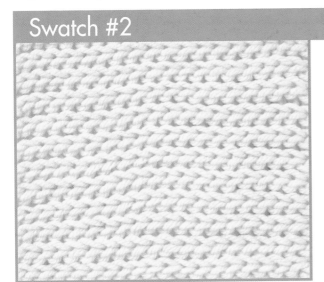

Knit: With yarn in back, insert hook from front to back in lp indicated, yo, pull through st and lp on hook.
Purl: With yarn in front, insert hook from back to front in lp indicated, yo, pull through st and lp on hook.

INSTRUCTIONS

KNIT BACK LOOP
Row 1: CO/BO (see Special Stitches) any number of sts, turn.
Row 2: Knit (see Special Stitches) in **back lps** (see Stitch Guide) across, turn.
Rep row 2 for pattern.

PURL FRONT LOOP
Row 1: CO/BO (see Special Stitches) any number of sts, turn.
Row 2: Purl (see Special Stitches) in **front lps** (see Stitch Guide) across, turn.
Rep row 2 for pattern. ■

Knit back loop is a mirror image of purl front loop. Work either set of instructions to create Swatch #2.

SPECIAL STITCHES
Cast On/Bind Off (CO/BO): See instructions and photos in Introduction on pages 6–8.

Swatch #3

Twisted knit front loop is a mirror image of twisted purl back loop. Work either set of instructions to create Swatch #3.

SPECIAL STITCHES

Cast On/Bind Off (CO/BO): See instructions and photos in Introduction on pages 6–8.

Twisted knit: With yarn in back, insert hook from front to back in lp indicated, yo, pull through st and lp on hook, turn hook completely around counterclockwise, twisting lp on hook.

Twisted purl: With yarn in front, insert hook from back to front in lp indicated, yo, pull through st and lp on hook, turn hook completely around counterclockwise, twisting lp on hook.

INSTRUCTIONS

TWISTED KNIT FRONT LOOP

Row 1: CO/BO (*see Special Stitches*) any number of sts, turn.

Row 2: Twisted knit (*see Special Stitches*) in

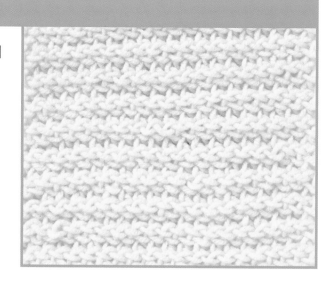

front lps (*see Stitch Guide*) across, turn.
Rep row 2 for pattern.

TWISTED PURL BACK LOOP

Row 1: CO/BO (*see Special Stitches*) any number of sts, turn.

Row 2: Twisted purl (*see Special Stitches*) in **back lps** (*see Stitch Guide*) across, turn.
Rep row 2 for pattern. ■

Swatch #4

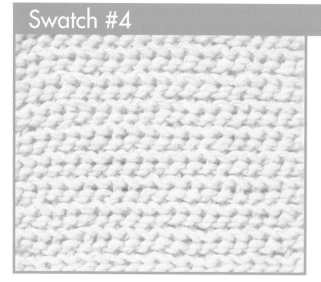

Twisted knit back loop is a mirror image of twisted purl front loop. Work either set of instructions to create Swatch #4.

SPECIAL STITCHES

Cast On/Bind Off (CO/BO): See instructions and photos in Introduction on pages 6–8.

Twisted knit: With yarn in back, insert hook from front to back in lp indicated, yo,

pull through st and lp on hook, turn hook completely around counterclockwise, twisting lp on hook.

Twisted purl: With yarn in front, insert hook from back to front in lp indicated, yo, pull through st and lp on hook, turn hook completely around counterclockwise, twisting lp on hook.

INSTRUCTIONS

TWISTED KNIT BACK LOOP

Row 1: CO/BO (*see Special Stitches*) any number of sts, turn.

Row 2: Twisted knit (*see Special Stitches*) in **back lps** (*see Stitch Guide*) across, turn.
Rep row 2 for pattern.

TWISTED PURL FRONT LOOP

Row 1: CO/BO (*see Special Stitches*) any number of sts, turn.

Row 2: Twisted Purl (*see Special Stitches*) in **front lps** (*see Stitch Guide*) across, turn.
Rep row 2 for pattern. ■

Hot Pad

SKILL LEVEL

EASY

FINISHED SIZE
7 inches square

MATERIALS
- Brown Sheep Lambs Pride Superwash medium (worsted) weight wool yarn (3½ oz/200 yds/99g per skein):
    1 skein #SW125 lemon ice
- Size J/10/6mm crochet hook or size needed to obtain gauge

GAUGE
10 sts = 2¾ inches; 19 rows = 4 inches

PATTERN NOTE
Join with slip stitch as indicated unless otherwise stated.

SPECIAL STITCHES
Cast On/Bind Off (CO/BO): See instructions and photos in Introduction on pages 6–8.
Twisted knit: With yarn in back, insert hook from front to back in lp indicated, yo, pull through st and lp on hook, turn hook completely around counterclockwise, twisting lp on hook.
Twisted purl: With yarn in front, insert hook from back to front in lp indicated, yo, pull through st and lp on hook, turn hook completely around counterclockwise, twisting lp on hook.
Knit: With yarn in back, insert hook from front to back in lp indicated, yo, pull through st and lp on hook.

INSTRUCTIONS

HOT PAD
Row 1 (RS): CO/BO (*see Special Stitches*) 27 sts, turn.
Row 2: Twisted purl (*see Special Stitches*) in 9 **back lps** (*see Stitch Guide*), **twisted knit** (*see*

Special Stitches) in 9 **front lps** (*see Stitch Guide*), twisted purl in 9 back lps, turn.
Next rows: Rep row 2 until piece measure 6¾ inches ending with WS row.

EDGING
Rnd 1 (RS): Working in front lps and in ends of rows, [evenly sp 22 **knit** (*see Special Stitches*) sts across ends of rows, ch 1 (*corner*)] around, **do not join.**
Rnd 2: [Knit in front lp of next st or ch, ch 1] around, **join** (*see Pattern Note*) in beg knit st. Fasten off. ■

STOCKINETTE STITCH

The biggest difference between knit and crochet, other than knitting uses 2 needles and crocheting uses 1 hook, is that in knitting the stitches remain on a knitting needle in an upright position and are generally only bound off the needle when the work is complete. In crochet, every time a stitch is made, the previous stitch is bound off. When a stitch is bound off, it lies in a horizontal position. Consequently, when using knitting needles, one creates vertical columns of stitches, and when one uses a crochet hook, one creates horizontal rows of stitches.

But as in all things, there are exceptions and ways around this, enabling one to create stitches with a crochet hook that look like vertical stockinette stitches, the most basic of knitting stitches created by working knit stitches on right side rows and working purl stitches on wrong side rows.

The easiest way of course, to make vertical columns of stockinette stitches, is to simply turn one's work sideways after it is complete. ■

Stockinette Stitch

SPECIAL STITCHES

Cast On/Bind Off (CO/BO): See instructions and photos in Introduction on pages 6–8.

Knit: With yarn in back, insert hook from front to back in lp indicated, yo, pull through st and lp on hook.

Purl: With yarn in front, insert hook from back to front in lp indicated, yo, pull through st and lp on hook.

INSTRUCTIONS

STOCKINETTE STITCH

Row 1 (RS): Working from side to side, **CO/BO** *(see Special Stitches)* any number of sts, turn.

Row 2: Purl *(see Special Stitches)* in **front lps** *(see Stitch Guide)* across, turn.

Row 3: Knit *(see Special Stitches)* in **back lps** *(see Stitch Guide)* across, turn.

Rep rows 2 and 3 for pattern. ■

Manipulated Stockinette Stitch

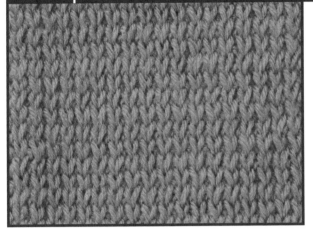

SPECIAL STITCHES

One can also manipulate the stitches in such a way that they appear to line up in vertical columns. This creates a dense fabric of stockinette stitches.

Cast On/Bind Off (CO/BO): See instructions and photos in Introduction on pages 6–8.

Knit: With yarn in back, insert hook from front to back in lp indicated, yo, pull through st and lp on hook.

Purl: With yarn in front, insert hook from back to front in lp indicated, yo, pull through st and lp on hook.

INSTRUCTIONS

MANIPULATED STOCKINETTE STITCH

Row 1 (RS): Working from bottom to top, CO/BO *(see Special Stitches)* any number of sts, turn.

Row 2: Purl *(see Special Stitches)* 1 in **back lp** *(see Special Stitches)*, [insert hook purl wise through back lp of next st, **front lp** *(see Stitch Guide)* of previous st, front lp of next st *(same st where one just inserted into the back lp)*, yo, pull through all 3 sts and lp on hook] across to last st, purl 1 in back lp, turn.

Row 3: Knit *(see Special Stitches)* 1 in front lp, [insert hook knit wise through front lp of next st, back lp of previous st, back lp of next st *(same st where one just inserted in front lp)*, yo, pull through all 3 sts and lp on hook] across to last st, knit 1 in front lp, turn.

Rep rows 2 and 3 for pattern. ■

Stockinette Sub Stitch

In order to knit cables with a crochet hook, one needs a stitch that not only runs vertically when worked from bottom to top, one also needs a stitch that will allow drape in the fabric. Although the next stitch doesn't have the appearance of stockinette, it is a good substitute for the stockinette stitch being that the stitch runs vertically and has the required drape to form cables. Thus, when working cables, this is generally the preferred stitch.

SPECIAL STITCHES

Cast On/Bind Off (CO/BO): See instructions and photos in Introduction on pages 6–8.

Knit: With yarn in back, insert hook from front to back in lp indicated, yo, pull through st and lp on hook.

Purl: With yarn in front, insert hook from back to front in lp indicated, yo, pull through st and lp on hook.

INSTRUCTIONS

STOCKINETTE SUB STITCH

Row 1 (RS): Working from bottom to top,

CO/BO *(see Special Stitches)* any number of sts, turn.

Row 2: Purl *(see Special Stitches)* in **back lps** *(see Stitch Guide)* across, turn.

Row 3: Knit *(see Special Stitches)* in **front lps** *(see Stitch Guide)* across, turn.

Rep rows 2 and 3 for pattern. ■

Reverse Stockinette Stitch

In knitting, the back side of stockinette, called reverse stockinette, shows the purl stitches. Purl stitches lie in horizontal rows. When working in stockinette with knitting needles, when one works a new stitch on the right needle, the loop from the left needle is dropped. Just as in crocheting, when a loop in knitting is dropped or bound off it goes into a horizontal position. Since the purl side of stockinette is conveniently already in horizontal

rows, to work the purl side, with crochet hook, one need do nothing more than simply turn the stockinette swatch over.

SPECIAL STITCHES
Cast On/Bind Off (CO/BO): See instructions and photos in Introduction on pages 6–8.
Knit: With yarn in back, insert hook from front to back in lp indicated, yo, pull through st and lp on hook.
Purl: With yarn in front, insert hook from back to front in lp indicated, yo, pull through st and lp on hook.

INSTRUCTIONS

REVERSE STOCKINETTE STITCH
Row 1 (WS): Working from bottom to top, **CO/BO** (*see Special Stitches*) any number of sts, turn.
Row 2: Purl (*see Special Stitches*) in **front lps** (*see Stitch Guide*) across, turn.
Row 3: Knit (*see Special Stitches*) in **back lps** (*see Stitch Guide*) across, turn.
Rep rows 2 and 3 for pattern. ■

Reverse Stockinette Sub Stitch

Although reverse stockinette lies down in perfect horizontal rows when worked from bottom to top, occasionally one might need horizontal rows of reverse stockinette stitches when working from side to side. The same substitute stitch used to make vertical stockinette from bottom to top can also be used to make horizontal reverse stockinette when working from side to side.

SPECIAL STITCHES
Cast On/Bind Off (CO/BO): See instructions and photos in Introduction on pages 6–8.
Knit: With yarn in back, insert hook from front to back in lp indicated, yo, pull through st and lp on hook.
Purl: With yarn in front, insert hook from back to front in lp indicated, yo, pull through st and lp on hook.

INSTRUCTIONS

REVERSE STOCKINETTE SUB STITCH
Row 1 (RS): Working from side to side, CO/BO

(*see Special Stitches*) any number of sts, turn.
Row 2: Purl (*see Special Stitches*) in **back lps** (*see Stitch Guide*) across, turn.
Row 3: Knit (*see Special Stitches*) in **front lps** (*see Stitch Guide*) across, turn.
Rep rows 2 and 3 for pattern. ■

Basket Weave Yarn Bag

SKILL LEVEL

INTERMEDIATE

FINISHED SIZE
4 x 10 x 11 inches, excluding handles

MATERIALS
- TLC Essentials medium (worsted) weight yarn (6 oz/312 yds/170g per skein): MEDIUM
    - 2 skeins #2254 persimmon
- Size K/10½/6.5mm crochet hook or size needed to obtain gauge
- Tapestry needle
- Sewing needle
- Sewing thread
- ⅜-inch wooden dowel rods: 2 12 inches long
- ⅜-inch hole wooden dowel caps: 4
- Wood glue
- 3¾ x 9½ x 10½-inch canvas bag with 1 x 16-inch handles #802900 Me &My B.A.G. by Barbara A. Green
- Large safety pin
- Stitch marker

GAUGE
19 sts = 5 inches; 24 rows = 5 inches

PATTERN NOTE
Join with slip stitch as indicated unless otherwise stated.

SPECIAL STITCHES
Cast On/Bind Off (CO/BO): See instructions and photos in Introduction on pages 6–8.
Knit: With yarn in back, insert hook from front to back in lp indicated, yo, pull through st and lp on hook.
Purl: With yarn in front, insert hook from back to front in lp indicated, yo, pull through st and lp on hook.

INSTRUCTIONS

BAG
SIDE
MAKE 2.
Row 1 (RS): Side is worked from side to side, **CO/BO** (see Special Stitches) 45 sts, mark last st as top of Bag, turn.

Row 2: Purl (see Special Stitches) 5 in front lps, [purl 5 in back lps, purl 5 in front lps] across, turn.
Row 3: Knit (see Special Stitches) 5 in back lps, [knit 5 in front lps, knit 5 in back lps] across, turn.
Rows 4–7: [Rep rows 2 and 3 alternately] twice.
Row 8: Purl 5 in back lps, [purl 5 in front lps, purl 5 in back lps] across, turn.
Row 9: Knit 5 in front lps, [knit 5 in back lps, knit 5 in front lps] across, turn.
Rows 10–13: [Rep rows 8 and 9 alternately] twice.
Rows 14–72: [Rep rows 2–13 consecutively] 5 times, ending last rep with row 12. At end of last row, fasten off.
Turn so marker is at top edge; piece should measure 11½ inches high and 15 inches wide.

ASSEMBLY
With RS facing, sew bottom seam.
Mark 2 inches from bottom of Bag on each side edge of Bag.
Tuck bottom 2 inches of Bag inside Bag between front and back layer accordion style so that the bottom 2 inches of the Bag is now 4 layers thick.
The marked stitches 2 inches from bottom on each

side are now at the very bottom of the Bag.
Sew side seams.
Turn RS out.

EDGING
Rnd 1: With RS facing, **join** (*see Pattern Note*) at top of Bag at side seam, evenly sp knit sts around top of Bag, **do not join.**
Rnd 2: Knit in back lp of each st around, join in back lp of beg knit st. Fasten off.

TOTE LINING
Turn canvas tote bag WS out so that the pockets are on the inside.
Carefully remove canvas tote handles and set aside.
Place tote inside Bag and sew in place around top edge.

STRAP
MAKE 2.

FIRST STRAP END
Row 1: Leaving long end at beg, CO/BO 5 sts, turn.
Row 2: Purl 5 in back lps, turn.
Row 3: Knit 5 in front lps, turn.
Rows 4–7: [Rep rows 2 and 3 alternately] twice.
Row 8: Rep row 2.

TUBE
Rnds 1 & 2: Now working in rnds, knit 5 in front lps, ch 5, being careful not to twist ch, knit in front lp of first st to form ring, knit 4 in front lps, knit in front lp of each ch, **do not join rnds,** mark first st of rnd.
Rnd 3: Knit in front lp of each st around.
Next rnds: Rep rnd 3 until piece measures 14½ inches from beg.
Using safety pin, pull canvas handle through Tube, leaving 1½ inches of handle extended out at each end of Tube.

2ND STRAP END
Row 1: Flatten Tube, knit in front lp of each st across until First Strap End is in back of work, turn.
Rows 2–9: [Rep rows 2 and 3 alternately of First Strap End] 4 times. At end of last row, leaving long end, fasten off.

ASSEMBLY
Glue wooden end cap to each end of wooden dowel rods.
Sew each end of canvas handle around dowel rod so that handle is centered on rod and handle ends are 5 inches apart.
Using long ends, sew each end of Strap around dowel rod and to Tube so that Strap is centered on rod and Strap ends are 5 inches apart.
Using yarn, sew dowel rods to center 10 inches of top of Bag in front and back. ■

Two-Toned Stockinette Scarf

SKILL LEVEL

EASY

FINISHED SIZE

5 x 61 inches, excluding Fringe

MATERIALS

■ Red Heart Super Saver medium (worsted) weight yarn (7 oz/364 yds/198g per skein):

1 skein each #313 Aran and #334 buff
■ Size L/11/8mm crochet hook or size needed to obtain gauge

GAUGE

14 sts = 5 inches; 20 rows = 5 inches

SPECIAL STITCHES

Cast On/Bind Off (CO/BO): See instructions and photos in Introduction on pages 6–8.

Knit: With yarn in back, insert hook from front to back in lp indicated, yo, pull through st and lp on hook.

Purl: With yarn in front, insert hook from back to front in lp indicated, yo, pull through st and lp on hook.

INSTRUCTIONS

SCARF

Row 1 (RS): Working from side to side, with Aran, **CO/BO** *(see Special Stitches)* 172 sts **changing colors** *(see Stitch Guide)* to buff in last st, working on opposite side of sts, **knit** *(see Special Stitches)* in each lp across, turn.

Row 2: **Purl** *(see Special Stitches)* in **front lps** *(see Stitch Guide)* across first 172 sts changing to Aran in last st, leaving rem sts unworked for bottom edge, turn.

Row 3: Knit in **back lps** *(see Stitch Guide)* across, turn.

Row 4: Purl in front lps across changing to buff in last st, turn.

Row 5: Knit in back lps across, turn.

Row 6: Purl in front lps across, changing to Aran in last st, turn.

Rows 7–18: [Rep rows 3–6 consecutively for pattern] 3 times.

Row 19: Rep row 3. Fasten off.

FRINGE

Cut 24 strands of Aran and 20 strands of buff each 10 inches long.

Holding 2 strands of same color tog, fold in half, insert hook from back to front through stitch, pull fold through st, pull ends through fold. Pull to tighten.

Matching colors, attach Fringe in each color change on each end of Scarf. ■

SHAPING

One shapes crochet work by increasing and/or decreasing the number of stitches in a row or round.

DECREASING & INCREASING SEVERAL STITCHES

When knitting and purling with a crochet hook, one can decrease several stitches at the end of a row by simply leaving the stitches unworked. If one needs to decrease several stitches at both ends of a row, such as when working decreases for armhole openings, one should work 2 rows, decreasing at the end of each.

Increasing several stitches is also done at the end of rows. To increase several stitches, work to the end of the row, then yarn over/bind off (YO/BO) the number of stitches one wants to add before turning the work. YO/BO are knitting terms that mean the same thing as chain 1. ■

Diamond—Increasing & Decreasing

SPECIAL STITCHES

Cast On/Bind Off (CO/BO): See instructions and photos in Introduction on pages 6–8.
Knit: With yarn in back, insert hook from front to back in lp indicated, yo, pull through st and lp on hook.
Purl: With yarn in front, insert hook from back to front in lp indicated, yo, pull through st and lp on hook.

INSTRUCTIONS

DIAMOND
DECREASING & INCREASING SEVERAL STITCHES

Row 1 (RS): Working from side to side, **CO/BO** *(see Special Stitches)* 2 sts, turn.
Row 2: Purl *(see Special Stitches)* in **front lps** *(see Stitch Guide)* across, ch 2 *(2 st inc)*, turn.
Row 3: Knit *(see Special Stitches)* in **back lps** *(see Stitch Guide)* across, ch 2 *(2 st inc)*, turn.
Rows 4–9: [Rep rows 2 and 3 alternately] 3 times. *(18 sts at end of last row)*
Row 10: Purl in front lps across, leaving last 2 sts unworked, turn.

Row 11: Knit in back lps across, leaving last 2 sts unworked, turn.
Rows 12–17: [Rep rows 10 and 11 alternately] 3 times. At end of last row, fasten off. *(2 sts at end of last row)* ■

DECREASING ONE STITCH

To decrease one stitch, work one stitch over two stitches.

Due to the nature of the knit and purl stitches, this is accomplished in two different ways depending on if one wants the stitches to slant to the left or if one wants the stitches to slant to the right.

To make a knit decrease so that the stitches slant to the left, work ssk.

When working a right-side row, this is generally the technique used for decreasing on the right-hand side of the fabric:

Slip slip knit (ssk): Insert hook knit wise in each of next two stitches, yarn over, pull through both stitches, then bind off by pulling through loop on hook. Stitch slants to the left.

To make a knit decrease so that the stitches slant to the right, work k2tog. When working a right-side row, this is generally the technique used for decreasing on the left-hand side of the fabric:

Knit two together (k2tog): Skip next stitch, insert hook knit wise through next stitch, then insert hook knit wise through skipped stitch, yarn over, pull through both stitches, then bind off by pulling through loop on hook. Stitch slants to the right.

To make a purl decrease on the wrong side so that the stitches slant to the left when the right side is facing, work ssp. When the wrong side is facing, this is generally the technique used for decreasing on the left-hand side of the fabric:

Slip slip purl (ssp): Worked on wrong-side rows, skip next stitch, insert hook purl wise through next stitch, then insert hook purl wise through skipped stitch, yarn over, pull through both stitches, then bind off by pulling through loop on hook. Stitch slants to the left when right side is facing.

To make a purl decrease on the wrong side so that the stitches slant to the right when the right side is facing, work p2tog. When the wrong side is facing, this is generally the technique used for decreasing on the right-hand side of the fabric:

Purl two together (p2tog): Worked on wrong-side rows, insert hook purl wise through each of next two stitches, yarn over, pull through both stitches and loop on hook. Stitch slants to the right when right side is facing. ∎

Triangle—Decreasing One Stitch

SPECIAL STITCHES

Cast On/Bind Off (CO/BO): See instructions and photos in Introduction on pages 6–8.

Knit: With yarn in back, insert hook from front to back in lp indicated, yo, pull through st and lp on hook.

Purl: With yarn in front, insert hook from back to front in lp indicated, yo, pull through st and lp on hook.

Purl 2 together (p2tog): See Decreasing One Stitch above.

Slip slip purl (ssp): See Decreasing One Stitch above.

Knit 2 together (k2tog): See Decreasing One Stitch above.

Slip slip knit (ssk): See Decreasing One Stitch above.

INSTRUCTIONS

TRIANGLE
DECREASING ONE STITCH

Row 1 (RS): Working from bottom to top, **CO/BO** (*see Special Stitches*) 20 sts, turn.

Row 2: P2tog *(see Special Stitches)* in **front lp** *(see Stitch Guide)*, **purl** *(see Special Stitches)* in front lps across to last 2 sts, **ssp** *(see Special Stitches)* in front lps, turn. *(18 sts)*

Row 3: Ssk *(see Special Stitches)* in **back lps** *(see Stitch Guide)*, **knit** *(see Special Stitches)* in back lps across to last 2 sts, **k2tog** *(see Special Stitches)* in back lps, turn. *(16 sts)*

Rows 4–9: [Rep rows 2 and 3 alternately] 3 times. *(4 sts at end of last row)*

Row 10: P2tog in front lps, ssp in front lps, turn. *(2 sts)*

Row 11: Ssk in back lps. Fasten off. ∎

INCREASING ONE STITCH

To increase one stitch, work one stitch between two stitches.

Just as in decreasing stitches, there are also two methods used to increase stitches depending on if one wants the stitches to slant to the left or if one wants the stitches to slant to the right.

To make a knit increase so that the stitches slant to the left, work M1K-L. When working a right-side row, this is generally the technique used for increasing on the left-hand side of the fabric:

Make one knit left (M1K-L): Insert hook knit wise through stitch just worked, then insert hook knit wise through next stitch, yarn over, pull through both stitches, then bind off by pulling through loop on hook.

To make a knit increase so that the stitches slant to the right, work M1K-R. When working a right-side row, this is generally the technique used for increasing on the right-hand side of the fabric:

Make one knit right (M1K-R): Insert hook knit wise through next stitch, then insert hook knit wise through previous stitch, yarn over, pull through both stitches, then bind off by pulling through loop on hook.

To make a purl increase on the wrong side so that the stitches slant to the left when the right side is facing, work M1P-L. When the wrong side is facing, this is generally the technique used for increasing on the right-hand side of the fabric:

Make one purl left (M1P-L): Worked on wrong-side rows, insert hook purl wise through next stitch, then insert hook purl wise through previous stitch, yarn over, pull through both stitches, then bind off by pulling through loop on hook. Stitch slants to the left when right side is facing.

To make a purl increase on the wrong side so that the stitches slant to the right when the right side is facing, work M1P-R. When the wrong side is facing, this is generally the technique used for increasing on the left-hand side of the fabric:

Make one purl right (M1P-R): Worked on wrong-side rows, insert hook purl wise through stitch just worked, then insert hook purl wise through next stitch, yarn over, pull through both stitches, then bind off by pulling through loop on hook. Stitch slants to the right when right side is facing. ∎

Circle—Increasing One Stitch

PATTERN NOTES
Work in continuous rounds, do not turn or join unless otherwise stated.
Mark first stitch of round.

SPECIAL STITCHES
Cast On/Bind Off (CO/BO): See instructions and photos in Introduction on pages 6–8.
Knit: With yarn in back, insert hook from front to back in lp indicated, yo, pull through st and lp on hook.
Make 1 knit right (M1K-R): See Increasing One Stitch article on page 24.

INSTRUCTIONS

CIRCLE
INCREASING ONE STITCH
Rnd 1 (RS): Working in rounds, **CO/BO** *(see Special Stitches)* 6 sts, **do not join** *(see Pattern Notes)*.
Rnd 2: Knit *(see Special Stitches)* in **back lp** *(see Stitch Guide)* of first st to form circle, knit 1 in back lp, [**M1K-R** *(see Special Stitches)* in back lps, knit 2 in back lps] twice. *(8 sts)*
Rnd 3: [M1K-R in back lps, knit 1 in back lp] 8 times. *(16 sts)*
Rnd 4: Knit in back lps around.
Rnd 5: [M1K-R in back lp, knit 2 in back lps] 8 times. *(24 sts)*

Rnd 6: Knit in back lps around.
Rnd 7: [M1K-R in back lps, knit 3 in back lps] 8 times. *(32 sts)*
Rnd 8: Knit in back lps around.
Rnd 9: [M1K-R in back lps, knit 4 in back lps] 8 times. *(40 sts)*
Rnd 10: Knit in back lps around.
Rnd 11: [M1K-R in back lps, knit 5 in back lps] 8 times. *(48 sts)*
Rnd 12: Knit in back lps around. Fasten off. ∎

Stockinette Cap

SKILL LEVEL

INTERMEDIATE

FINISHED SIZES

Instructions given fit child's 10¼ inches high, excluding Pompom x 18 inches circumference *(small)*; changes for adult 12 inches high, excluding Pompom x 20 inches circumference *(medium)* are in [ ].

MATERIALS

- Red Heart Classic medium (worsted) weight yarn (3½ oz/190 yds/99g per skein): 1 [1] skein #827 light periwinkle
- Size L/11/8mm crochet hook or size needed to obtain gauge
- Tapestry needle
- Pompom maker

GAUGE

12 sts = 4 inches; 16 rows = 4 inches
Take time to check gauge.

SPECIAL STITCHES

Cast On/Bind Off (CO/BO): See instructions and photos in Introduction on pages 6–8.

Knit: With yarn in back, insert hook from front to back in lp indicated, yo, pull through st and lp on hook.

Purl: With yarn in front, insert hook from back to front in lp indicated, yo, pull through st and lp on hook.

INSTRUCTIONS

CAP

Row 1 (WS): CO/BO *(see Special Stitches)* 32 [36] sts, turn.

Row 2: Knit *(see Special Stitches)* 30 [34] in **back lps** *(see Stitch Guide)*, leaving rem sts unworked, turn.

Row 3: Purl *(see Special Stitches)* 16 [18] in **front lps** *(see Stitch Guide)*, knit 14 [16] in back lps, turn.

Row 4: Knit 28 [32] in back lps, leaving rem sts unworked, turn.

Row 5: Purl 14 [16] in front lps, knit 14 [16] in back lps, turn.

Row 6: Knit 26 [30] in back lps, leaving rem sts unworked, turn.

Row 7: Purl 12 [14] in front lps, knit 14 [16] in back lps, turn.

Row 8: This row works sts from bottom of Cap all the way to top of Cap, knit 26 [30] in back lps, [insert hook knit wise in end of row, then insert hook knit wise in back lp of unworked st on row below, yo, pull through both sts and lp on hook, knit 1 in back lp] 3 times, turn. (32 [36] sts)

Row 9: Purl 18 [20] in front lps, knit 14 [16] in back lps, turn.

Rows 10–72 [10–80]: [Rep rows 2–9 consecutively] 8 [9] times for pattern, ending last rep with row 8. At end of last row, leaving long end, fasten off.

FINISHING

Weave long end through row ends at top of Cap, pull tight to close. Place cast-on row and last row side-by-side with WS facing up. Weave long end through back of stitches of cast-on row and last row, effectively sewing the 2 rows tog.

POMPOM

Make 2-inch Pompon with pompon maker.
Attach Pompom to top of Cap.
Fold cuff in half to right side. ∎

LACE

Knitted lace worked with knitting needles is produced in several ways.

One method is to do a yarn over so that there is an unworked stitch which produces an opening in the fabric. This is followed by a slip 1, knit 1, pass slipped stitch over, creating a one-stitch decrease so that the number of stitches remains the same on the row.

ANALYSIS

When working with a crochet hook, one binds off the previous stitch (*the loop on the hook*) when the next stitch is made (*the consequence of pulling the new stitch through the loop on the hook*).

Therefore, when crocheting a knit yarn over, one is actually working a chain stitch (*wrap yarn around hook then pull through loop on hook*).

To work a slip 1, knit 1, psso in crochet, one inserts the hook into the next stitch knit wise (*slip 1*), then inserts the hook into the next stitch knit wise, does a yarn over and pulls the loop through the stitch (*knit 1*), then pulls the loop through the slipped stitch (*psso*), then, since in crochet previous stitches are bound off when new stitches are formed, the loop is pulled through the loop on the hook.

Therefore, when crocheting a slip 1, knit 1, psso, one is actually working a crocheted knit decrease (*insert hook in each of next two stitches, yarn over, pull through both stitches and loop on hook*).

To form knit lace with a crochet hook using this knitting method, one simply needs to make a chain stitch or two, depending on the size opening one desires, followed by decreasing an equal number of stitches so that the stitch count on the row remains the same. ∎

Turkish Lace

Slip 1, Knit 1, pass slipped stitch over (slip 1, knit 1, psso): Insert hook knit wise in front lp of next st (*sl 1*), insert hook knit wise in front lp of next st, yo, pull through st and also through st that was sl (*knit 1, psso*), then bind off by pulling through lp on hook.

INSTRUCTIONS

TURKISH LACE
Row 1 (RS): Working from bottom to top, **CO/BO** (*see Special Stitches*) even number of sts, turn.
Row 2: Knit (*see Special Stitches*) 1 in **front lp** (*see Stitch Guide*), [yo (*ch 1*), **sl 1, knit 1, psso** (*see Special Stitches*)] across, ending with knit 1 in front lp of last st, turn.
Rep row 2 for pattern. ∎

SPECIAL STITCHES
Cast On/Bind Off (CO/BO): See instructions and photos in Introduction on pages 6–8.
Knit: With yarn in back, insert hook from front to back in lp indicated, yo, pull through st and lp on hook.

K2tog Lace

If one works Turkish Lace using the k2tog decrease method, instead of the slip 1, knit 1, psso method, one will get a totally different look.

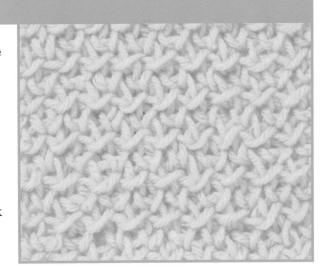

SPECIAL STITCHES
Cast On/Bind Off (CO/BO): See instructions and photos in Introduction on pages 6–8.
Knit: With yarn in back, insert hook from front to back in lp indicated, yo, pull through st and lp on hook.
Knit 2 together (k2tog): Sk next st, insert hook knit wise through next st, then insert hook knit wise through sk st, yo, pull through both sts and lp on hook.

INSTRUCTIONS

K2TOG LACE
Row 1 (RS): Working from bottom to top, **CO/ BO** (*see Special Stitches*) even number of sts, turn.

Row 2: Knit (*see Special Stitches*) 1 in **front lp** (*see Stitch Guide*), [ch 1, **k2tog** (*see Special Stitches*)] across, ending with knit last st in front lp, turn.
Rep row 2 for pattern. ■

Scalloped Lace

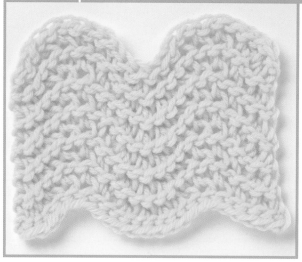

The yarn over increase, decrease method can also be used to create lacy-shaped pieces.

SPECIAL STITCHES

Cast On/Bind Off (CO/BO): See instructions and photos in Introduction on pages 6–8.

Knit: With yarn in back, insert hook from front to back in lp indicated, yo, pull through st and lp on hook.

Knit 2 together (k2tog): Sk next st, insert hook knit wise through next st, then insert hook knit wise through sk st, yo, pull through both sts and lp on hook.

INSTRUCTIONS

SCALLOPED LACE

Row 1 (RS): Working from bottom to top, **CO/BO** (*see Special Stitches*) in a multiple of 12 sts, turn.

Row 2: Knit (*see Special Stitches*) in back lps across, turn.

Row 3: *[K2tog (*see Special Stitches*) in front lps] twice, [ch 1, knit 1 in front lp] 4 times, [k2tog in front lps] twice, rep from * across, turn.

Stitch count will rem the same, there is an increase for every decrease.

Rep rows 2 and 3 alternately for pattern. ∎

Puffed Lace Ribbing

A second method for producing knit lace with knitting needles is by working several stitches into one stitch. The loop, that the stitches are worked into, puffs up to hold the extra stitches creating an opening. This is followed by decreasing stitches on the row to maintain the stitch count.

SPECIAL STITCHES

Cast On/Bind Off (CO/BO): See instructions and photos in Introduction on pages 6–8.

Knit: With yarn in back, insert hook from front to back in lp indicated, yo, pull through st and lp on hook.

Purl: With yarn in front, insert hook from back to front in lp indicated, yo, pull through st and lp on hook.

INSTRUCTIONS

PUFFED LACE RIBBING

Row 1 (RS): Working from bottom to top, **CO/BO** (*see Special Stitches*) in a multiple of 4 sts plus 2, turn.

Row 2: Knit (*see Special Stitches*) 1 in **back lp** (*see Stitch Guide*), [yif (*yarn in front*), insert hook knit wise in back lp of next st, purl wise in back

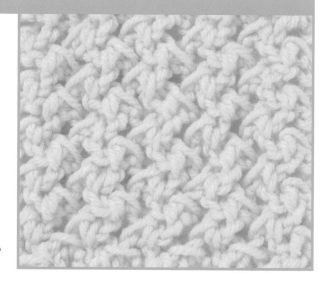

lp of next st, knit wise in back lp of next st, bring yarn from front to back over, then under hook, pull through all 3 sts and lp on hook turning hook counterclockwise (*1 st made using 3 sts*), (knit, **purl**–*see Special Stitches*, knit) in back lp of next st (*3 sts made using 1 st*)] across, ending with knit 1 in back lp of last st, turn.

Row 3: Purl 1 in **front lp** (*see Stitch Guide*), [yib (*yarn in back*), insert hook purl wise in front lp of next st, knit wise in front lp of next st, purl wise in front lp of next st, bring yarn from back to front over, then under hook, pull through all 3 sts and lp on hook turning hook clockwise (*1 st made using 3 sts*), (purl, knit, purl) in front lp of next st (*3 sts made using 1 st*)] across to last st, purl in front lp of last st, turn.

Rep rows 2 and 3 alternately for pattern. ∎

Ribbed Lace

One can also lace the ribs themselves by working the lacy openings directly onto the rib panels.

SPECIAL STITCHES

Cast On/Bind Off (CO/BO): See instructions and photos in Introduction on pages 6–8.

Knit: With yarn in back, insert hook from front to back in lp indicated, yo, pull through st and lp on hook.

Purl: With yarn in front, insert hook from back to front in lp indicated, yo, pull through st and lp on hook.

Knit 2 together (k2tog): Sk next st, insert hook knit wise through next st, then insert hook knit wise through sk st, yo, pull through both sts and lp on hook.

INSTRUCTIONS

RIBBED LACE

Row 1 (RS): Working from bottom to top, **CO/BO** (*see Special Stitches*) in a multiple of 9 sts plus 6, turn.

Row 2: Purl (*see Special Stitches*) 2 in **back lps** (*see Stitch Guide*), [knit 2 in **front lps** (*see Stitch Guide*), purl 7 in back lps] across to last 4 sts, knit 2 in front lps, purl last 2 in back lps, turn.

Row 3: Knit (*see Special Stitches*) 2 in front lps, [purl 2 in back lps, **k2tog** (*see Special Stitches*) in front lps, ch 2, yib (*yarn in back*), insert hook knit wise in front lp of next st, purl wise in front lp of next st, knit wise in front lp of next st, yo, pull through all 3 sts and lp on hook (*1 st made using 3 sts*), ch 2, k2tog in front lps] across to last 4 sts, purl 2 in back lps, knit last 2 in front lps, turn.

Rep rows 2 and 3 alternately for pattern. ∎

Dropped Stitch Lace

A third method for producing knit lace with knitting needles is to knit a stitch, wrapping the yarn around the needle two or three times instead of once. On the following row, the knit stitches are worked and the wrapped loops are dropped. When the row is completed, the dropped loops are allowed to go up to their natural height, leaving a lacy appearance.

To do the dropped loop lace method with a crochet hook, wrap the yarn around the hook two or three times, insert the hook in the next stitch, yarn over, pull through the stitch, remove the loop just pulled through from the hook, let the wrapped loops drop to the back of the work, insert hook back into the loop that was removed, then bind off by pulling it through the loop on the hook. Be careful not to allow loops to pull up to their natural height until the following row is completed.

The crochet hook dropped loop method can be worked from bottom to top making the reverse stockinette side the front of the fabric, or it can be worked from side to side making the stockinette side the front of the fabric.

SPECIAL STITCHES
Cast On/Bind Off (CO/BO): See instructions and photos in Introduction on pages 6–8.
Knit: With yarn in back, insert hook from front to back in lp indicated, yo, pull through st and lp on hook.
Purl: With yarn in front, insert hook from back to front in lp indicated, yo, pull through st and lp on hook.
Dropped stitch: Wrap yarn around hook twice, insert hook in back lp of next st, yo, pull through st, remove the lp just pulled through

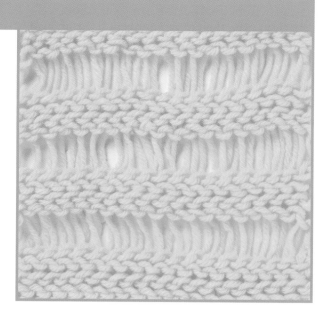

from the hook, let the wrapped lps drop to the back of the work, insert hook back in the lp that was removed, then pull through lp on hook.

INSTRUCTIONS

DROPPED STITCH LACE
Row 1: CO/BO *(see Special Stitches)* any number of sts, turn.
Row 2: Purl *(see Special Stitches)* in **front lps** *(see Stitch Guide)* across, turn.
Row 3: Knit *(see Special Stitches)* in **back lps** *(see Stitch Guide)* across, turn.
Row 4: Purl in front lps across, turn.
Row 5: Dropped stitch *(see Special Stitches)* across, after last st on row is worked, drop lp from hook, insert hook purl wise through same back lp just worked, pull dropped lp through, turn.
Rep rows 2–5 consecutively for pattern. ∎

Staggered Lace Scarf

SKILL LEVEL

INTERMEDIATE

FINISHED SIZE
6 x 52 inches

MATERIALS
- Red Heart Super Saver medium (worsted) weight yarn (7 oz/364 yds/198g per skein):
  1 skein #327 light coral
- Size M/13/9mm crochet hook or size needed to obtain gauge

GAUGE
11 sts = 3 inches; 23 rows = 6 inches

SPECIAL STITCHES
Cast On/Bind Off (CO/BO): See instructions and photos in Introduction on pages 6–8.
Knit: With yarn in back, insert hook from front to back in lp indicated, yo, pull through st and lp on hook.
Slip slip slip knit (sssk): Insert hook knit wise in front lp of each of next 3 sts, yo, pull through all 3 sts and lp on hook.

INSTRUCTIONS

SCARF
Row 1 (WS): CO/BO *(see Special Stitches)* 22 sts, turn.
Row 2: Knit *(see Special Stitches)* in **front lps** *(see Stitch Guide)* across, turn.
Row 3: Knit in **back lps** *(see Stitch Guide)* across, turn.
Row 4: Knit 1 in front lp, [ch 2, **sssk** *(see Special Stitches)*] across, turn.
Row 5: Rep row 3.
Rows 6 & 7: Rep rows 2 and 3.
Row 8: [Sssk, ch 2] across, ending with knit 1 in front lp of last st, turn.
Row 9: Rep row 3.
Next rows: Rep rows 2–9 for pattern until piece measure 52 inches from beg, ending with row 4 or row 8. At end of last row, fasten off.
Last row: Working on opposite side of row 1, join with sl st in first st, knit 1 in front lp of same st, [ch 2, sssk] across. Fasten off. ■

RIBBING

When knitting and purling with a crochet hook, one can work ribbing from side to side or from bottom to top.

The method for side-to-side ribbing gives a nice stretchy material that simulates the look of knitted ribbing. ■

Side-to-Side Ribbing

SPECIAL STITCHES

Cast On/Bind Off (CO/BO): See instructions and photos in Introduction on pages 6–8.
Knit: With yarn in back, insert hook from front to back in lp indicated, yo, pull through st and lp on hook.

INSTRUCTIONS

SIDE-TO-SIDE RIBBING

Row 1 (WS): Working from side to side, **CO/BO** (*see Special Stitches*) any number of sts, mark last st as bottom of ribbing, turn.
Row 2: Knit (*see Special Stitches*) in **back lps** (*see Stitch Guide*) across, turn.
Rep row 2 for pattern. ■

Twisted Purl Ribbing

Although not as stretchy as when crocheting knit into the back lp of sts, one can make a pretty ribbing by working twisted purl in back lp of sts.

SPECIAL STITCHES

Cast On/Bind Off (CO/BO): See instructions and photos in Introduction on pages 6–8.
Twisted purl: With yarn in front, insert hook from back to front in lp indicated, yo, pull through st and lp on hook, turn hook completely around counterclockwise, twisting lp on hook.

INSTRUCTIONS

TWISTED PURL RIBBING

Row 1 (WS): Working from side to side, **CO/BO** (*see Special Stitches*) any number of sts, mark last st as bottom of ribbing, turn.
Row 2: Twisted purl (*see Special Stitches*) in **back lps** (*see Stitch Guide*) across, turn.
Rep row 2 for pattern. ■

Knit Ribbing Alternating Loops

For a little something different, one can also form side-to-side ribs by alternating front and back loops. This ribbing has about the same amount of stretch as Twisted Purl Ribbing.

SPECIAL STITCHES

Cast On/Bind Off (CO/BO): See instructions and photos in Introduction on pages 6–8.

Knit: With yarn in back, insert hook from front to back in lp indicated, yo, pull through st and lp on hook.

INSTRUCTIONS

KNIT RIBBING USING ALTERNATING LOOPS

Row 1 (WS): Working from side to side, CO/BO (*see Special Stitches*) odd number of sts, mark last st as bottom of ribbing, turn.

Row 2: Knit (*see Special Stitches*) 1 in **front lp** (*see Stitch Guide*), [knit 1 in **back lp** (*see Stitch Guide*), knit 1 in front lp] across, turn.

Rep row 2 for pattern. ■

1-by-1 Ribbing

When working ribbing from bottom to top, the more stitches worked, the more stretch the fabric has. 3-by-3 ribbing has a lot of stretch compared to 1-by-1 ribbing.

SPECIAL STITCHES

Cast On/Bind Off (CO/BO): See instructions and photos in Introduction on pages 6–8.

Purl: With yarn in front, insert hook from back to front in lp indicated, yo, pull through st and lp on hook.

Knit: With yarn in back, insert hook from front to back in lp indicated, yo, pull through st and lp on hook.

INSTRUCTIONS

1-BY-1 RIBBING

Row 1 (RS): Working from bottom to top, CO/BO (*see Special Stitches*) even number of sts, turn.

Row 2: [Purl (*see Special Stitches*) 1 in **back lp** (*see Stitch Guide*), knit (*see Special Stitches*) 1 in **front lp** (*see Stitch Guide*)] across, turn.

Rep row 2 for pattern. ■

2-by-2 Ribbing

SPECIAL STITCHES
Cast On/Bind Off (CO/BO): See instructions and photos in Introduction on pages 6–8.

Knit: With yarn in back, insert hook from front to back in lp indicated, yo, pull through st and lp on hook.
Purl: With yarn in front, insert hook from back to front in lp indicated, yo, pull through st and lp on hook.

INSTRUCTIONS

2-BY-2 RIBBING
Row 1 (RS): Working from bottom to top, **CO/BO** (*see Special Stitches*) a multiple of 4 sts plus 2, turn.
Row 2: **Purl** (*see Special Stitches*) 2 in **back lps** (*see Stitch Guide*), [**knit** (*see Special Stitches*) 2 in **front lps** (*see Stitch Guide*), purl 2 in back lps] across, turn.
Row 3: Knit 2 in front lps, [purl 2 in back lps, knit 2 in front lps] across, turn.
Rep rows 2 and 3 alternately for pattern. ■

3-by-3 Ribbing

SPECIAL STITCHES
Cast On/Bind Off (CO/BO): See instructions and photos in Introduction on pages 6–8.
Knit: With yarn in back, insert hook from front to back in lp indicated, yo, pull through st and lp on hook.
Purl: With yarn in front, insert hook from back to front in lp indicated, yo, pull through st and lp on hook.

INSTRUCTIONS

3-BY-3 RIBBING
Row 1 (RS): Working from bottom to top, **CO/BO** (*see Special Stitches*) a multiple of 6 sts plus 3, turn.
Row 2: **Purl** (*see Special Stitches*) 3 in **back lps** (*see Stitch Guide*), [**knit** (*see Special Stitches*) 3 in **front lps** (*see Stitch Guide*), purl 3 in back lps] across, turn.

Row 3: Knit 3 in front lps, [purl 3 in back lps, knit 3 in front lps] across, turn.
Rep rows 2 and 3 alternating for pattern. ■

Mistake Ribbing

One can also work knitted Mistake Ribbing with a crochet hook. This ribbing has little stretch, but forms almost perfect vertical columns.

SPECIAL STITCHES

Cast On/Bind Off (CO/BO): See instructions and photos in Introduction on pages 6–8.

Knit: With yarn in back, insert hook from front to back in lp indicated, yo, pull through st and lp on hook.

Purl: With yarn in front, insert hook from back to front in lp indicated, yo, pull through st and lp on hook.

INSTRUCTIONS

MISTAKE RIBBING

Row 1 (RS): Working from bottom to top, **CO/BO** *(see Special Stitches)* in a multiple of 4 sts plus 3, turn.

Row 2: [**Knit** *(see Special Stitches)* 2 in **front lps** *(see Stitch Guide)*, **purl** *(see Special Stitches)* 2 in **back lps** *(see Stitch Guide)*] across to last 3 sts, knit 2 in front lps, purl 1 in back lps of last st, turn.

Rep row 2 for pattern. ■

Child's Ribbed Skirt

SKILL LEVEL

INTERMEDIATE

FINISHED SIZES

Instructions given fit child's size 4 (small); changes for size 6 (medium), size 8 (large) and size 10 (X-large) are in [ ].

FINISHED GARMENT MEASUREMENTS

Length: 10 inches (small) [11½ inches (medium), 12½ inches (large), 14 inches (X-large)]

MATERIALS

- Red Heart Classic medium (worsted) weight yarn (3½ oz/190 yds/99g per skein): 2 [2, 2, 3] skeins #615 artichoke

- Size L/11/8mm crochet hook or size needed to obtain gauge
- Tapestry needle
- Sewing needle
- Matching sewing thread
- ½-inch elastic: 21½ [22½, 23½, 24½] inches

GAUGE

15 sts = 6 inches; 18 rows = 6 inches
Take time to check gauge.

SPECIAL STITCHES

Cast On/Bind Off (CO/BO): See instructions and photos in Introduction on pages 6–8.

Knit: With yarn in back, insert hook from front to back in lp indicated, yo, pull through st and lp on hook.

Purl: With yarn in front, insert hook from back to front in lp indicated, yo, pull through st and lp on hook.

Knit 2 together (k2tog): Sk next st, insert hook knit wise through next st, then insert hook knit wise through sk st, yo, pull through both sts and lp on hook.

Slip Slip purl (sl sl purl): Sk next st, insert hook purl wise through next st, then insert hook purl

wise through sk st, yo, pull through both sts and lp on hook.

INSTRUCTIONS

SKIRT

Row 1 (WS): CO/BO (see Special Stitches) 150 (160, 180, 190) sts, turn.

Row 2 (RS): [Purl (see Special Stitches) 5 in **back lps** (see Stitch Guide), **knit** (see Special Stitches) 5 in **front lps** (see Stitch Guide)] across, turn.

Next rows: Rep row 2 for pattern until piece measures 3 (3½, 4, 4½) inches from beg, ending with WS row.

Next row (dec row RS): [Purl 2 in back lps, **sl sl purl** (see Special Stitches) in back lps, purl 1 in back lp, knit 2 in front lps, **k2tog** (see Special Stitches) in front lps, knit 1 in front lp] across, turn. (120 [128, 144, 152] sts)

Next rows: Continue working in pattern until piece measures 6 [7, 8, 9] inches from beg, ending with WS row.

Next row (dec row RS): [Purl 1 in back lp, sl sl purl in back lps, purl 1 in back lp, knit 1 in front lp, k2tog in front lps, knit 1 in front lp] across, turn. (90 [96, 108, 114] sts)

Next rows: Continue working in established pattern until piece measures 9 [10½, 11½, 13] inches from beg, ending with WS row.

Next row (dec row RS): [Purl 1 in back lp, sl sl purl in back lps, knit in 1 front lp, k2tog in front lps] across, turn. (60 [64, 72, 76] sts)

WAISTBAND

Row 1 (WS): Knit in back lps across, turn.

Row 2: Purl in front lps across, turn.

Rows 3–6: [Rep rows 1 and 2 alternately] twice. At end of last row, leaving long end, fasten off.

FINISHING

With RS facing, sew back seam.
Overlap ends of elastic 1 inch to form circle, sew tog. Fold Waistband in half, placing elastic inside fold. Sew Waistband row 6 to Waistband row 1, encasing elastic inside. ∎

TEXTURED STITCHES

Working knit and purl stitches with a crochet hook lends as many stitch combinations, if not more, than using knitting needles. Thus, the texture possibilities are numerous.

Here are just a few.

Garter Stitch

SPECIAL STITCHES

Cast On/Bind Off (CO/BO): See instructions and photos in Introduction on pages 6–8.

Knit: With yarn in back, insert hook from front to back in lp indicated, yo, pull through st and lp on hook.

INSTRUCTIONS

GARTER STITCH

Row 1 (RS): Working from bottom to top, **CO/BO** (*see Special Stitches*) any number of sts, turn.

Row 2: Knit (*see Special Stitches*) in **back lps** (*see Stitch Guide*) across, turn.

Row 3: Knit in **front lps** (*see Stitch Guide*) across, turn.

Rep rows 2 and 3 for pattern. ∎

Tracks

SPECIAL STITCHES

Cast On/Bind Off (CO/BO): See instructions and photos in Introduction on pages 6–8.

Knit: With yarn in back, insert hook from front to back in lp indicated, yo, pull through st and lp on hook.

Purl: With yarn in front, insert hook from back to front in lp indicated, yo, pull through st and lp on hook.

INSTRUCTIONS

TRACKS SWATCH

Row 1 (RS): Working from bottom to top, **CO/BO** (*see Special Stitches*) multiple of 8 sts plus 4, turn.

Row 2: Purl (*see Special Stitches*) in **back lps** (*see Stitch Guide*) across, turn.

Row 3: Knit (*see Special Stitches*) 4 in **front lps** (*see Stitch Guide*), [purl 4 in front lps, knit 4 in front lps] across, turn.

Row 4: Rep row 2.

Row 5: Purl 4 in front lps, [knit 4 in front lps, purl 4 in front lps] across, turn.

Rep rows 2–5 consecutively for pattern. ∎

SEED STITCH:

To make 1-by-1 ribbing, one works rows of alternating knit and purl stitches whereby one knits the purl stitches and purls the knit stitches. Seed stitch is just the opposite. To form seed stitch, one works rows alternating knit and purl stitches where one knits the knit stitches and purls the purl stitches.

When working seed stitch with a crochet hook, one can create two different textures.

If the knit stitches are worked in front loops and the purl stitches are worked in the back loops, the end result is a pretty fabric with baby soft seeds.

If the knit stitches are worked in the back loops and the purl stitches are worked in the front loops, the end result is a bold, tactile fabric.

Baby Bear Seed Stitch

Knit: With yarn in back, insert hook from front to back in lp indicated, yo, pull through st and lp on hook.

Purl: With yarn in front, insert hook from back to front in lp indicated, yo, pull through st and lp on hook.

INSTRUCTIONS

BABY BEAR SEED STITCH

Row 1 (RS): Working from bottom to top, **CO/BO** (*see Special Stitches*) odd number of sts, turn.

Row 2: Knit (*see Special Stitches*) 1 in **front lp** (*see Stitch Guide*), [purl 1 in **back lp** (*see Stitch Guide*), knit 1 in front lp] across, turn.

Rep row 2 for pattern. ∎

SPECIAL STITCHES

Cast On/Bind Off (CO/BO): See instructions and photos in Introduction on pages 6–8.

Papa Bear Seed Stitch

SPECIAL STITCHES

Cast On/Bind Off (CO/BO): See instructions and photos in Introduction on pages 6–8.

Knit: With yarn in back, insert hook from front to back in lp indicated, yo, pull through st and lp on hook.

Purl: With yarn in front, insert hook from back to front in lp indicated, yo, pull through st and lp on hook.

INSTRUCTIONS

PAPA BEAR SEED STITCH

Row 1 (RS): Working from bottom to top, **CO/BO** (*see Special Stitches*) odd number of sts, turn.

Row 2: Knit (*see Special Stitches*) 1 in **back lp** (*see Stitch Guide*), [**purl** (*see Special Stitches*) 1

in **front lp** (*see Stitch Guide*), knit 1 in back lp] across, turn.

Rep row 2 for pattern. ∎

Bow Tie

SPECIAL STITCHES

Cast On/Bind Off (CO/BO): See instructions and photos in Introduction on pages 6–8.

Knit: With yarn in back, insert hook from front to back in lp indicated, yo, pull through st and lp on hook.

Purl: With yarn in front, insert hook from back to front in lp indicated, yo, pull through st and lp on hook.

Bow: Yib *(yarn in back)*, [insert hook purl wise in back lp of next st *(2 lps on hook)*, pass 2nd lp on hook over first lp *(1 lp on hook)*] 5 times,

yif *(yarn in front)* leaving free strand formed in back fairly loose.

Knot: Insert hook from bottom to top under 3 free strands below, then knit 1 in front lp of next st so that free strands are caught up in st.

INSTRUCTIONS

BOW TIE

Row 1 (RS): Working from bottom to top, **CO/BO** *(see Special Stitches)* in a multiple of 10 sts plus 7, turn.

Row 2: Purl *(see Special Stitches)* in **back lps** *(see Stitch Guide)* across, turn.

Row 3: Knit *(see Special Stitches)* in **front lps** *(see Stitch Guide)* across, turn.

Row 4: Purl 1 in back lp, [**bow** *(see Special Stitches)*, purl 5 in back lps] across to last 6 sts, bow, purl 1 in back lp, turn.

Rows 5–8: [Rep rows 3 and 4 alternately] twice.

Row 9: Knit 3 in front lps, [**knot** *(see Special Stitches)*, knit 9 in front lps] across to last 4 sts, knot, knit 3 in front lps, turn.

Row 10: Rep row 2.

Row 11: Rep row 3.

Row 12: Purl 6 in back lps, [bow, purl 5 in back lps] across to last st, purl last st in back lp, turn.

Rows 13–16: [Rep rows 11 and 12 alternately] twice.

Row 17: Knit 8 in front lps, [knot, knit 9 in front lps] across to last 9 sts, knot, knit 8 in front lps, turn.

Rep rows 2–17 consecutively for pattern. ∎

Herringbone

SPECIAL STITCH
Cast On/Bind Off (CO/BO): See instructions and photos in Introduction on pages 6–8.

INSTRUCTIONS

HERRINGBONE
Row 1 (RS): Working from side to side, **CO/BO** *(see Special Stitch)* any number of sts, turn.
Row 2: [Yif *(yarn in front)*, insert hook knit wise in back lp of next st, bring yarn from front to back over, then under hook, pull through st and lp on hook turning hook counterclockwise] across, turn.
Row 3: [Yib *(yarn in back)*, insert hook purl wise in front lp of next st, bring yarn from back to front over, then under hook, pull through st and lp on hook turning hook clockwise] across, turn.
Rep rows 2 and 3 alternately for pattern. ■

Gathered Stitch

Purl: With yarn in front, insert hook from back to front in lp indicated, yo, pull through st and lp on hook.
Purl 2 together (p2tog): Insert hook purl wise through each of next two stitches, yarn over, pull through both stitches and loop on hook.

INSTRUCTIONS

GATHERED STITCH
Row 1 (WS): Working from bottom to top, **CO/ BO** *(see Special Stitches)* any number of sts, turn.
Row 2: **Purl** *(see Special Stitches)* in **front lps** *(see Stitch Guide)* across, turn.
Row 3: **Knit** *(see Special Stitches)* in **back lps** *(see Stitch Guide)* across, turn.
Row 4: Knit in front lp and knit in back lp of each st across, turn. There are now twice as many sts as at beg.
Row 5: Purl in back lps across, turn.
Row 6: Knit in front lps across, turn.
Row 7: Rep row 5.
Row 8: [P2tog *(see Special Stitches)* in front lps] across, turn.
There are now the same amount of sts as on row 1.
Row 9: Rep row 3.
Rep rows 2–9 consecutively for pattern. ■

SPECIAL STITCHES
Cast On/Bind Off (CO/BO): See instructions and photos in Introduction on pages 6–8.
Knit: With yarn in back, insert hook from front to back in lp indicated, yo, pull through st and lp on hook.

Pick-Up Stitch

SPECIAL STITCHES

Cast On/Bind Off (CO/BO): See instructions and photos in Introduction on pages 6–8.

Knit: With yarn in back, insert hook from front to back in lp indicated, yo, pull through st and lp on hook.

Purl: With yarn in front, insert hook from back to front in lp indicated, yo, pull through st and lp on hook.

Purl 2 together (p2tog): Insert hook purl wise through each of next 2 sts, yo, pull through both sts and lp on hook.

Slip slip knit (ssk): Insert hook knit wise in each of next 2 sts, yo, pull through both sts, then bind off by pulling through lp on hook.

INSTRUCTIONS

PICK-UP STITCH

Row 1 (RS): Working from bottom to top, CO/BO *(see Special Stitches)* in a multiple of 5 sts plus 4, turn.

Row 2: Knit *(see Special Stitches)* 4 in **back lps** *(see Stitch Guide)*, [knit 1 in front lp, knit 4 in back lps] across, turn.

Row 3: Purl *(see Special Stitches)* 4 in **front lps** *(see Stitch Guide)*, [knit in front lp of st on row 1 pulling st up even with current row *(this creates 1 st inc)*, **p2tog** *(see Special Stitches)* in front lps, purl 3 in front lps] across, turn.

Row 4: Knit in back lps across, turn.

Row 5: Purl 4 in front lps, [yib *(yarn in back)*, insert hook purl wise from right to left under post of knit inc st 2 rows below, yo, pull through the post and up even with current row then pull through lp on hook *(1 st inc)*, p2tog in front lps, purl 3 in front lps] across, turn.

Row 6: Rep row 4.

Row 7: Purl 4 in front lps, [yib, insert hook purl wise from right to left under 4 strands that make up the post of inc st 2 rows below, yo, pull through the 4 strands and up even with the current row then pull through lp on hook *(1 st inc)*, p2tog in front lps *(1 st dec)*, purl 3 in front lps] across, turn.

Next rows: Rep rows 6 and 7 for pattern until piece measures 1 row less than desired length ending with RS row.

Last row (WS): Knit 4 in back lps, [yif *(yarn in front)*, insert hook in back, purl wise from right to left, under the 4 strands that make up the post of the inc st, yo, pull through the 4 strands and the lp on hook *(1 st inc)*, **ssk** *(see Special Stitches)* in back lps *(1 st dec)*, knit 3 in back lps] across. Fasten off. ∎

Pseudo 1-By-1 Ribbing Stitch

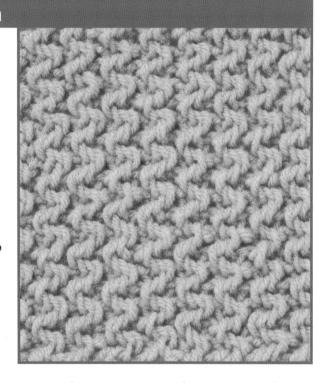

Pseudo 1-by-1 Ribbing produces the same look as 1-by-1 Ribbing. It works well for a texture stitch due to the design appearing only on the front of the fabric, which reduces the elasticity that creates the ribbing effect.

SPECIAL STITCHES

Cast On/Bind Off (CO/BO): See instructions and photos in Introduction on pages 6–8.

Knit: With yarn in back, insert hook from front to back in lp indicated, yo, pull through st and lp on hook.

Purl: With yarn in front, insert hook from back to front in lp indicated, yo, pull through st and lp on hook.

INSTRUCTIONS

PSEUDO 1-BY-1 RIBBING STITCH

Row 1 (RS): Working from bottom to top, **CO/BO** *(see Special Stitches)* even number of sts, turn.

Row 2: [**Knit** *(see Special Stitches)* 1 in **back lp** *(see Stitch Guide)*, **purl** *(see Special Stitches)* 1 in back lp] across, turn.

Row 3: [Knit 1 in **front lp** *(see Stitch Guide)*, purl 1 in front lp] across, turn.

Rep rows 2 and 3 alternately for pattern. ■

Smocking

SPECIAL STITCHES
Cast On/Bind Off (CO/BO): See instructions and photos in Introduction on pages 6–8.

Knit: With yarn in back, insert hook from front to back in lp indicated, yo, pull through st and lp on hook.

Purl: With yarn in front, insert hook from back to front in lp indicated, yo, pull through st and lp on hook.

INSTRUCTIONS

SMOCKING
Row 1 (RS): Working from side to side, **CO/BO** *(see Special Stitches)* in a multiple of 4 sts plus 3, turn.

Row 2: Purl *(see Special Stitches)* in **front lps** *(see Stitch Guide)* across, turn.

Row 3: Knit *(see Special Stitches)* in front lps across, turn.

Rep rows 2 and 3 alternately for pattern.

HONEYCOMB SMOCKING
Turn piece so that there are vertical columns of raised lps. Number the columns from left to right.

Thread tapestry needle. Beg at bottom left corner, insert needle from back to front, to left of first raised lp in column 1. Insert needle from right to left under first lp in column 2, then under first loop in column 1. Insert needle from front to back to the right of the first lp in column 2. Sk next 3 raised lps going up column 1, insert needle from back to front to the left of next raised lp in column 1. Insert needle from right to left under corresponding lp in column 2, then under lp in column 1. Insert needle from front to back to the right of the lp just worked in column 2.

Continue in same manner until 2 lps remain in column 1.

Insert needle from back to front to the left of the top raised lp in column 2. Insert needle from right to left under top raised lp in column 3, then under top raised lp in column 2. Insert needle from front to back to the right of the top lp in column 3.

Sk next 3 raised lps going down column 2, insert needle from back to front, to the left of the next raised lp in column 2. Insert needle from right to left under corresponding lp in column 3, then under lp in column 2. Insert needle from front to back to the right of the lp just worked in column 3.

Continue in same manner smocking each column of raised lps. ■

Duplicate Stitch

SPECIAL STITCHES

Cast On/Bind Off (CO/BO): See instructions and photos in Introduction on pages 6–8.

Knit: With yarn in back, insert hook from front to back in lp indicated, yo, pull through st and lp on hook.

Purl: With yarn in front, insert hook from back to front in lp indicated, yo, pull through st and lp on hook.

INSTRUCTIONS

DUPLICATE STITCH

Row 1 (RS): Working from side to side, **CO/BO** (*see Special Stitches*) in a multiple of 11 sts, turn.

Row 2: Purl (*see Special Stitches*) in **front lps** (*see Stitch Guide*) across, turn.

Row 3: Knit (*see Special Stitches*) in **back lps** (*see Stitch Guide*) across, turn.

Rep rows 2 and 3 alternately for pattern.

DUPLICATE STITCH

Thread tapestry needle. Insert needle from back to front through piece at bottom of V where duplicate stitch is to be worked. Insert needle from right to left under V st above. Insert needle from front to back through same place where duplicate stitch began (*see Fig. 1*).

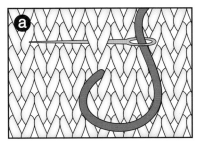

Fig. 1
Duplicate Stitch

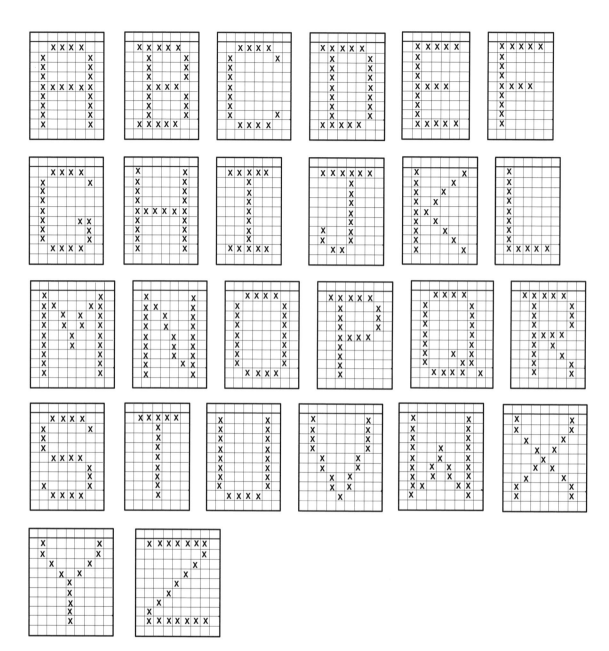

Duplicate Stitch
Alphabet Chart

Stripes

SPECIAL STITCHES

Cast On/Bind Off (CO/BO): See instructions and photos in Introduction on pages 6–8.

Knit: With yarn in back, insert hook from front to back in lp indicated, yo, pull through st and lp on hook.

Purl: With yarn in front, insert hook from back to front in lp indicated, yo, pull through st and lp on hook.

INSTRUCTIONS

STRIPES

Row 1 (RS): Working from bottom to top, **CO/BO** (*see Special Stitches*) any number of sts, turn.

Row 2: Purl (*see Special Stitches*) in **front lps** (*see Special Stitches*) across, turn.

Row 3: Knit (*see Special Stitches*) in **back lps** (*see Special Stitches*) across, turn.

Row 4: Rep row 2.

Row 5: Knit in front lps across, turn.

Row 6: Purl in back lps across, turn.

Row 7: Rep row 3.

Rows 8 & 9: Rep rows 2 and 3.

Row 10: Rep row 6.

Row 11: Knit in front lps across, turn.

Rep rows 2–11 consecutively for pattern.∎

Twisted Garter

Knit: With yarn in back, insert hook from front to back in lp indicated, yo, pull through st and lp on hook.

Twisted purl: With yarn in front, insert hook from back to front in lp indicated, yo, pull through st and lp on hook, turn hook completely around counterclockwise, twisting lp on hook.

INSTRUCTIONS

TWISTED GARTER

Row 1 (RS): Working from bottom to top, **CO/BO** (*see Special Stitches*) any number of sts, turn.

Row 2: Twisted purl (*see Special Stitches*) in **back lps** (*see Stitch Guide*) across, turn.

Row 3: Knit (*see Special Stitches*) in back lps across, turn.

Rep rows 2 and 3 alternately for pattern. ∎

SPECIAL STITCHES

Cast On/Bind Off (CO/BO): See instructions and photos in Introduction on pages 6–8.

Stockinette Basket Weave

There are several ways to produce the famous basket weave look.

To work a stockinette basket weave one can use the stockinette stitch for the vertical strips and use the reverse stockinette sub stitch for the horizontal strips.

The woven design appears on the front side of the work only.

SPECIAL STITCHES

Cast On/Bind Off (CO/BO): See instructions and photos in Introduction on pages 6–8.

Knit: With yarn in back, insert hook from front to back in lp indicated, yo, pull through st and lp on hook.

Purl: With yarn in front, insert hook from back to front in lp indicated, yo, pull through st and lp on hook.

INSTRUCTIONS

STOCKINETTE BASKET WEAVE

Row 1 (RS): Working from side to side, **CO/BO** *(see Special Stitches)* in a multiple of 10 sts plus 5, mark last st as top of work, turn.

Row 2: Purl *(see Special Stitches)* 5 in **front lps** *(see Stitch Guide)*, [purl 5 in **back lps** *(see Stitch Guide)*, purl 5 in front lps] across, turn.

Row 3: Knit *(see Special Stitches)* 5 in back lps, [knit 5 in front lps, knit 5 in back lps] across, turn.

Rows 4–7: [Rep rows 2 and 3 alternately] twice.

Row 8: Purl 5 in back lps, [purl 5 in front lps, purl 5 in back lps] across, turn.

Row 9: Knit 5 in front lps, [knit 5 in back lps, knit 5 in front lps] across, turn.

Rows 10–13: [Rep rows 8 and 9 alternately] twice.

Rep rows 2–13 consecutively for pattern. ∎

Sub Basket Weave

To work a basket weave that can be made from bottom to top or from side to side, and also a basket weave where the design appears on both sides of the work, one can use the stockinette substitute/reverse stockinette substitute stitches.

SPECIAL STITCHES

Cast On/Bind Off (CO/BO): See instructions and photos in Introduction on pages 6–8.

Knit: With yarn in back, insert hook from front to back in lp indicated, yo, pull through st and lp on hook.

Purl: With yarn in front, insert hook from back to front in lp indicated, yo, pull through st and lp on hook.

INSTRUCTIONS

SUB BASKET WEAVE

Row 1: Working from bottom to top or side to side, **CO/BO** (see Special Stitches) a multiple of 10 sts plus 5, turn.

Row 2: **Purl** (see Special Stitches) 5 in back lps, [**knit** (see Special Stitches) 5 in **front lps** (see Stitch Guide), purl 5 in **back lps** (see Stitch Guide)] across, turn.

Row 3: Knit 5 in front lps, [purl 5 in back lps, knit 5 in front lps] across, turn.

Rows 4–7: [Rep rows 2 and 3 alternately] twice.

Row 8: Knit 5 in front lps, [purl 5 in back lps, knit 5 in front lps] across, turn.

Row 9: Purl 5 in back lps, [knit 5 in front lps, purl 5 in back lps] across, turn.

Rows 10–13: [Rep rows 8 and 9 alternately] twice.

Rep rows 2–13 consecutively for pattern. ∎

Herringbone Pillow

SKILL LEVEL

INTERMEDIATE

FINISHED SIZE
12 x 16 inches

MATERIALS
- Red Heart Super Saver medium (worsted) weight yarn (7 oz/364 yds/198g per skein):
  1 skein #336 warm brown
- Sizes H/8/5mm and L/11/8mm crochet hooks or size needed to obtain gauge
- 12 x 16-inch pillow form

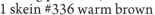

4 MEDIUM

GAUGE
Size L hook: 11 sts = 3 inches; 10 rows = 4 inches

SPECIAL STITCHES
Cast On/Bind Off (CO/BO): See instructions and photos in Introduction on pages 6–8.

Knit: With yarn in back, insert hook from front to back in lp indicated, yo, pull through st and lp on hook.

Purl: With yarn in front, insert hook from back to front in lp indicated, yo, pull through st and lp on hook.

INSTRUCTIONS

COVER
Row 1 (RS): Worked from side to side, with size L hook, **CO/BO** (*see Special Stitches*) 44 sts, turn.

Row 2: [Yif (*yarn in front*), insert hook knit wise in back lp of next st, bring yarn from front to back over then under hook, pull through st and lp on hook turning hook counterclockwise] across, turn.

Row 3: [Yib (*yarn in back*), insert hook purl wise in front lp of next st, bring yarn from back to front over then under hook, pull through st and lp on hook turning hook clockwise] across, turn.

Next rows: Rep rows 2 and 3 for pattern until piece measures 33 inches from beg.

Ribbing row: [**Purl** (*see Special Stitches*) 2 in back lps, **knit** (*see Special Stitches*) 2 in front lps] across, turn.

Next rows: Rep Ribbing row until piece measures 34½ inches from beg. At end of last row, fasten off.

ASSEMBLY
Place piece on flat surface with RS facing. Fold top or ribbing end 9¼ inches down then fold bottom edge 9¼ inches up with the 2 ends overlapping 2½ inches with bottom non-ribbed edge on top. Sew side seams.

Turn Cover RS out.

TASSEL BAND

MAKE 4.
With size H hook, CO/BO 10 sts. Fasten off. Sew first and last sts tog to form ring.

TASSELS

MAKE 4.
Cut 10 strands each 9 inches in length. Cut 1 strand 15 inches in length and securely tie the 10 strands tog around center. Fold in half.

Pull ends of 15 inch strand through center of Tassel Band pull Tassel Band over top of Tassel so that the Tassel Band is ½ inch from top of fold. Tie ends of 15 inch strand in knots until there is ½ inch of knots. Trim Tassel ends.

FINISHING
Place pillow form inside Cover.
Attach 1 Tassel to each corner of Pillow. ∎

Scrunch Pillow

SKILL LEVEL

INTERMEDIATE

FINISHED SIZE

14 inches square

MATERIALS

- Red Heart Super Saver medium (worsted) weight yarn (5 oz/260 yds/141g per skein):
  2 skeins #4313 Aran fleck
- Size L/11/8mm crochet hook or size needed to obtain gauge
- 14-inch square pillow form
- Tapestry needle

4 MEDIUM

GAUGE

15 sts = 5 inches; 22 rows = 5 inches

SPECIAL STITCHES

Cast On/Bind Off (CO/BO): See instructions and photos in Introduction on pages 6–8.

Knit: With yarn in back, insert hook from front to back in lp indicated, yo, pull through st and lp on hook.

Purl: With yarn in front, insert hook from back to front in lp indicated, yo, pull through st and lp on hook.

Purl 2 together (p2tog): Insert hook purl wise through each of next two stitches, yo, pull through both stitches and loop on hook.

INSTRUCTIONS

COVER

BOTTOM BACK

Row 1 (WS): CO/BO (see Special Stitches) 42 sts, turn.

Row 2: Purl (see Special Stitches) in **front lps** (see Stitch Guide) across, turn.

Row 3: Knit (see Special Stitches) in **back lps** (see Stitch Guide) across, turn.

Next rows: Rep rows 2 and 3 alternately until piece measures 9¼ inches from beg, ending with row 3.

FRONT

Row 1: Knit in front lp and knit in back lp of each st across, turn. (84 sts)

Row 2: Purl in back lps across, turn.

Row 3: Knit in front lps across, turn.

Row 4: Purl in back lps across, turn.

Row 5: [P2tog (see Special Stitches) in front lps] across, turn. (42 sts)

Row 6: Knit in back lps across, turn.

Row 7: Purl in front lps across, turn.

Row 8: Knit in back lps across, turn.

Rows 9–48: [Rep rows 1–8 of Front consecutively] 5 times.

TOP BACK

Next rows: Rep rows 2 and 3 of Bottom Back alternately until piece measures 29 inches from beg, ending with row 3.

RIBBING

Row 1: Knit 2 in front lps, [purl 2 in back lps, knit 2 in front lps] across, turn.

Row 2: Purl 2 in back lps, [knit 2 in front lps, purl 2 in back lps] across, turn.

Next rows: Rep rows 2 and 3 of Ribbing alternately until piece measures 30½ inches from beg. At end of last row, fasten off.

FINISHING

Place piece on flat surface with RS facing.

Fold ribbing end 8¼ inches down then fold bottom edge up 8¼ inches overlapping ends 2½ inches with bottom edge on top.

Sew side seams.

Turn Cover RS out.

Place pillow form in Cover. ■

Pick-Up Pillow

SKILL LEVEL

■■■□
INTERMEDIATE

FINISHED SIZE
15 inches in diameter

MATERIALS
- Red Heart Super Saver medium (worsted) weight yarn (5 oz/260 yds/141g per skein): 2 skeins #4334 buff fleck
- Size L/11/8mm crochet hook or size needed to obtain gauge
- 15-inch round pillow form
- Tapestry needle
- 13/16-inch round buttons: 2
- Stitch marker

GAUGE
Rnds 1–7 = 3 inches in diameter

PATTERN NOTES
Work in continuous rounds, do not turn or join unless otherwise stated.

Mark first stitch of round.

SPECIAL STITCHES
Cast On/Bind Off (CO/BO): See instructions and photos in Introduction on pages 6–8.

Knit: With yarn in back, insert hook from front to back in lp indicated, yo, pull through st and lp on hook.

Purl: With yarn in front, insert hook from back to front in lp indicated, yo, pull through st and lp on hook.

Pick up stitch (pick up st): Yib (*yarn in back*), insert hook purl wise from right to left under the 4 strands that make up the post of the inc st 3 rnds below, yo, pull through the 4 strands and up even with current row then pull through lp on hook (*1 st inc*).

INSTRUCTIONS
COVER
SIDE
MAKE 2.
Rnd 1 (RS): CO/BO (*see Special Stitches*) 6 sts, **do not join** (*see Pattern Notes*).

Rnd 2: Knit (*see Special Stitches*) in **back lp** (*see Stitch Guide*) of first st, then knit in **front lp** (*see Stitch Guide*) of same st, [knit in back lp of next st, then knit in front lp of same st] around. (*12 sts*)

Rnd 3: Knit in back lp of each st around.

Rnd 4: Purl (*see Special Stitches*) in front lp of each st around.

Rnd 5: [Knit in front lp of st on rnd 2 pulling st up even with current row (*inc*), purl 1 in front lp on this rnd] around. (*24 sts*)

Rnds 6 & 7: Rep rnd 4.

Rnd 8: [Pick up st (*see Special Stitches*), purl 2 in front lps on this rnd] around. (*36 sts*)

Rnds 9 & 10: Rep rnd 4.

Rnd 11: [Pick up st, purl 3 in front lps on this rnd] around. (*48 sts*)

Rnds 12 & 13: Rep rnd 4.

Rnd 14: [Pick up st, purl 4 in front lps on this rnd] around. (*60 sts*)

Rnds 15 & 16: Rep rnd 4.

Rnd 17: [Pick up st, purl 5 in front lps on this rnd] around. (*72 sts*)

Rnds 18 & 19: Rep rnd 4.

Rnd 20: [Pick up st, purl 6 in front lps on this rnd] around. (*84 sts*)

Rnds 21 & 22: Rep rnd 4.

Rnd 23: [Pick up st, purl 7 in front lps on this rnd] around. (*96 sts*)

Rnds 24 & 25: Rep rnd 4.

Rnd 26: [Pick up st, purl 8 in front lps on this rnd] around. (*108 sts*)

Rnds 27 & 28: Rep rnd 4.

Rnd 29: [Pick up st, purl 9 in front lps on this rnd] around. (*120 sts*)

Rnds 30 & 31: Rep rnd 4.

Rnd 32: [Pick up st, purl 10 in front lps on this rnd] around. (*132 sts*)

Rnds 33 & 34: Rep rnd 4.

Rnd 35: [Pick up st, purl 11 in front lps on this rnd] around. Fasten off. (*144 sts*)

FINISHING
Matching inc sts on Sides, sew Side pieces tog inserting pillow form before closing.

Holding 1 button at center top and 1 button at center bottom, sew buttons tog creating slight indent in pillow Sides. ■

BOBBLE

Bobbles and knots create a bumpy texture on the fabric. Knit bobbles and knots can be made with a crochet hook in same way they are made with knitting needles.

A bobble is the knit version of crocheted cluster. It is made by working several stitches into one using both the front and back loop of the stitch. The work is turned, and the newly created stitches are worked across. The work is turned again, and the extra stitches are decreased back into one stitch. After a bobble is made, one continues working stitches across the row. ■

Bobble

SPECIAL STITCHES

Cast On/Bind Off (CO/BO): See instructions and photos in Introduction on pages 6–8.

Knit: With yarn in back, insert hook from front to back in lp indicated, yo, pull through st and lp on hook.

Purl: With yarn in front, insert hook from back to front in lp indicated, yo, pull through st and lp on hook.

Bobble: (Knit in front lp, knit in back lp) twice in next st *(4 sts in 1)*, **turn**, purl 4 in back lps, **turn**, insert hook knit wise in front lp of next 4 sts, yo, pull through all 4 sts and lp on hook, push bobble to front of work and pull yarn slightly to tighten.

INSTRUCTIONS

BOBBLE

Row 1 (WS): Working from bottom to top, **CO/BO** *(see Special Stitches)* in a multiple of 4 sts plus 3, turn.

Row 2: Purl *(see Special Stitches)* in **front lps** *(see Stitch Guide)* across, turn.

Row 3: Knit *(see Special Stitches)* in **back lps** *(see Stitch Guide)* across, turn.

Row 4: Purl 3 in front lps, [**bobble** *(see Special Stitches)*, purl 3 in front lps] across, turn.

Row 5: Knit 3 in back lps, [knit 1 in back lp of bobble, knit 3 in back lps] across, turn.

Rows 6 & 7: Rep rows 2 and 3.

Row 8: Purl 5 in front lps, [bobble, purl 3 in front lps] across to last 2 sts, purl in front lp of last 2 sts, turn.

Row 9: Knit 5 in back lps, [knit in back lp of bobble, knit 3 in back lps] across to last 2 sts, knit in back lp of last 2 sts, turn.

Rep rows 2–9 for pattern. ■

Popcorn

A popcorn is worked the same as a bobble except that the added stitches are decreased back into one in such a way that only the first and last stitch are closed together.

SPECIAL STITCHES

Cast On/Bind Off (CO/BO): See instructions and photos in Introduction on pages 6–8.

Knit: With yarn in back, insert hook from front to back in lp indicated, yo, pull through st and lp on hook.

Purl: With yarn in front, insert hook from back to front in lp indicated, yo, pull through st and lp on hook.

Popcorn (pc): (Knit in front lp, {knit in back lp, knit in front lp} twice) in next st *(5 sts in 1)*, **turn**, purl 5 in back lps, **turn**, insert hook knit wise in front lp of next 2 sts *(3 lps on hook)*, pass 2nd lp on hook over first lp *(2 lps on hook)*, [insert hook knit wise in front lp of next st *(3 lps on hook)*, pass 2nd lp on hook over first lp *(2 lps on hook)*] 3 times, pushing popcorn to front of work, pass 2nd lp on hook over first lp, closing popcorn *(1 lp on hook)*.

INSTRUCTIONS

POPCORN

Row 1 (WS): Working from bottom to top, **CO/BO** *(see Special Stitches)* in a multiple of 5 sts, turn.

Row 2: Purl *(see Special Stitches)* in **front lps** *(see Stitch Guide)* across, turn.

Row 3: Knit *(see Special Stitches)* in **back lps** *(see Stitch Guide)* across, turn.

Row 4: [Purl 2 in front lps, **pc** *(see Special Stitches)*, purl 2 in front lps] across, turn.

Row 5: [Knit 2 in back lps, knit in back lp of pc, knit 2 in back lps] across, turn.

Rows 6 & 7: Rep rows 2 and 3.

Rep rows 2–7 consecutively for pattern. ∎

Puff

A puff begins on one row and is completed on the following row. It is opened by working several stitches into one using the front and back loop of the stitch, then closed on the next row by decreasing the extra stitches so that once again there is only one stitch.

SPECIAL STITCHES

Cast On/Bind Off (CO/BO): See instructions and photos in Introduction on pages 6–8.

Knit: With yarn in back, insert hook from front to back in lp indicated, yo, pull through st and lp on hook.

Purl: With yarn in front, insert hook from back to front in lp indicated, yo, pull through st and lp on hook.

Open puff: (Knit in front lp, knit in back lp) twice in next st *(4 sts in 1)*.

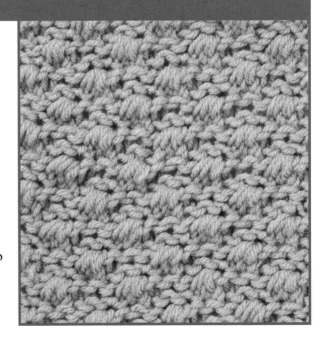

Close puff: Yif *(yarn in front)*, insert hook knit wise in back lp of next 4 sts, bring yarn from front to back over, then under hook, pull through all 4 sts and lp on hook.

INSTRUCTIONS

PUFF
Row 1 (WS): Working from bottom to top, **CO/ BO** *(see Special Stitches)* a multiple of 4 sts plus 3, turn.
Row 2: Purl *(see Special Stitches)* 1 in **front lp** *(see Stitch Guide)*, [**open puff** *(see Special Stitches)*, purl 3 in front lps] across to last 2 sts, open puff, purl 1 in front lp of last st, turn.
Row 3: Knit *(see Special Stitches)* 1 in **back lp** *(see Stitch Guide)*, [**close puff** *(see Special Stitches)*, knit 3 in back lps] across to last 2 sts, close puff, knit 1 in back lp of last st, turn.
Row 4: Purl 3 in front lps, [open puff, purl 3 in front lps] across, turn.
Row 5: Knit 3 in back lps, [close puff, knit 3 in back lps] across, turn.
Rep rows 2–5 consecutively for pattern. ∎

Hazelnut

The hazelnut is worked in the same way as the puff except that several rows are worked before the hazelnut is closed.

SPECIAL STITCHES
Cast On/Bind Off (CO/BO): See instructions and photos in Introduction on pages 6–8.
Knit: With yarn in back, insert hook from front to back in lp indicated, yo, pull through st and lp on hook.
Purl: With yarn in front, insert hook from back to front in lp indicated, yo, pull through st and lp on hook.
Open hazelnut: (Knit in front lp, {knit in back lp, knit in front lp} twice) in next st *(5 sts in 1)*.
Close hazelnut: Insert hook knit wise in front lp of next 5 sts, yo, pull through all 5 sts and lp on hook.

INSTRUCTIONS

HAZELNUT
Row 1 (WS): Working from bottom to top, **CO/ BO** *(see Special Stitches)* in a multiple of 6 sts plus 5, turn.
Row 2: Purl *(see Special Stitches)* in **front lps** *(see Stitch Guide)* across, turn.
Row 3: Knit *(see Special Stitches)* in **back lps** *(see Stitch Guide)* across, turn.

Row 4: Purl 5 in front lps, [**open hazelnut** *(see Special Stitches)*, purl 5 in front lps] across, turn.
Row 5: Knit 5 in back lps, [purl 5 in back lps, knit 5 in back lps] across, turn.
Row 6: Purl 5 in front lps, [knit 5 in front lps, purl 5 in front lps] across, turn.
Row 7: Rep row 5.
Row 8: Purl 5 in front lps, [**close hazelnut** *(see Special Stitches)*, purl 5 in front lps] across, turn.
Row 9: Rep row 3.
Rep rows 2–9 consecutively for pattern. ∎

Embedded River Rocks-Pebbles

Rocks and Pebbles, also known as knots, is a pattern that creates a different design on the front and back. One side is Embedded River Rocks and the other side is Pebbles. It is created by inserting the hook and pulling the yarn through the front and back loop of one stitch several times before pulling the last loop through all of the loops on the hook. When working the stitch, rocks appear on the front side of work and pebbles appear on the back side of work.

SPECIAL STITCHES

Cast On/Bind Off (CO/BO): See instructions and photos in Introduction on pages 6–8.

Knit: With yarn in back, insert hook from front to back in lp indicated, yo, pull through st and lp on hook.

Purl: With yarn in front, insert hook from back to front in lp indicated, yo, pull through st and lp on hook.

Rock: [Insert hook knit wise in front lp, yo, pull through st, insert hook knit wise in back lp, yo pull through st] twice in next st, insert hook knit wise in front lp of same st, yo, pull through st and all 5 lps on hook.

INSTRUCTIONS

EMBEDDED RIVER ROCKS/PEBBLES

Row 1: Working from bottom to top, **CO/BO** (*see Special Stitches*) a multiple of 4 sts plus 3, turn.

Row 2: Purl (*see Special Stitches*) in **back lps** (*see Stitch Guide*) across, turn.

Row 3: Knit (*see Special Stitches*) 1 in **front lp** (*see Stitch Guide*), [**rock** (*see Special Stitches*), knit 3 in front lps] across to last 2 sts, rock, knit 1 in front lp of last st, turn.

Row 4: Rep row 2.

Row 5: Knit 3 in front lps, [rock, knit 3 in front lps] across, turn.

Rep rows 2–5 consecutively for pattern. ■

Flower Garden Blankie

SKILL LEVEL

INTERMEDIATE

FINISHED SIZE
26 x 36 inches

MATERIALS
- Red Heart Classic medium (worsted) weight yarn (3½ oz/190 yds/99g per skein):
    4 skeins #579 light lavender
- Size L/11/8mm crochet hook or size needed to obtain gauge
- Sewing needle
- Matching sewing thread
- ⅜-inch-wide double-face ribbon: 5 yds light orchid

GAUGE
16 sts = 5 inches; 14 rows = 4 inches

SPECIAL STITCHES
Cast On/Bind Off (CO/BO): See instructions and photos in Introduction on pages 6–8.

Knit: With yarn in back, insert hook from front to back in lp indicated, yo, pull through st and lp on hook.

Purl: With yarn in front, insert hook from back to front in lp indicated, yo, pull through st and lp on hook.

Seed Border: Knit 1 in front lp, [purl 1 in back lp, knit 1 in front lp] 7 times.

Open petal: (Knit in front lp, {knit in back lp, knit in front lp} twice) in next st (*5 sts in 1*).

Close petal: Insert hook knit wise in front lp of next 5 sts, yo, pull through all 5 sts and lp on hook.

Bobble: (Knit in front lp, knit in back lp) twice in next st (*4 sts in 1*), turn, purl 4 in back lps, turn, insert hook knit wise in front lp of next 4 sts, yo, pull through all 4 sts and lp on hook, push bobble to front of work and pull yarn slightly to tighten.

INSTRUCTIONS

BLANKIE
Row 1 (RS): CO/BO (*see Special Stitches*) 83 sts, turn.

Rows 2–16: Knit (*see Special Stitches*) 1 in **front lp** (*see Stitch Guide*), [**purl** (*see Special Stitches*) 1 in **back lp** (*see Stitch Guide*), knit 1 in front lp] across, turn.

Row 17: Seed border (*see Special Stitches*), purl 53 in front lps, seed border, turn.

Row 18: Seed border, knit 53 in back lps, seed border, turn.

Rows 19–24: [Rep rows 17 and 18 alternately] 3 times.

Row 25: Seed border, purl 10 in front lps, **open petal** (*see Special Stitches*), [purl 15 in front lps, open petal] twice, purl 10 in front lps, seed border, turn. (*95 sts*)

Row 26: Seed border, knit 10 in back lps, purl 5 in back lps, [knit 15 in back lps, purl 5 in back lps] twice, knit 10 in back lps, seed border, turn.

Row 27: Seed border, purl 10 in front lps, knit 5 in front lps, [purl 15 in front lps, knit 5 in front lps] twice, purl 10 in front lps, seed border, turn.

Row 28: Rep row 26.

Row 29: Seed border, purl 7 in front lps, [open petal, purl 2 in front lps, **close petal** (*see Special Stitches*), purl 2 in front lps, open petal, purl 9 in front lps] twice, open petal, purl 2 in front lps, close petal, purl 2 in front lps, open petal, purl 7 in front lps, seed border, turn. (*107 sts*)

Row 30: Seed border, knit 7 in back lps, [purl 5 in back lps, knit 5 in back lps, purl 5 in back lps, knit 9 in back lps] twice, purl 5 in back lps, knit 5 in back lps, purl 5 in back lps, knit 7 in back lps, seed border, turn.

Row 31: Seed border, purl 7 in front lps, [knit 5 in front lps, purl 2 in front lps, **bobble** (*see Special Stitches*), purl 2 in front lps, knit 5 in front lps, purl 9 in front lps] twice, knit 5 in front lps, purl 2 in front lps, bobble, purl 2 in front lps, knit 5 in front lps, purl 7 in front lps, seed border, turn.

Row 32: Seed border, knit 7 in back lps, [purl 5 in back lps, knit 2 in back lps, knit in back lp of bobble, knit 2 in back lps, purl 5 in back lps, knit 9 in back lps] twice, purl 5 in back lps, knit 2 in back lps, knit in back lp of bobble, knit 2 in back lps, purl 5 in back lps, knit 7 in back lps, seed border, turn.

Row 33: Seed border, purl 7 in front lps, [close petal, purl 2 in front lps, open petal, purl 2 in front lps, close petal, purl 9 in front lps] twice, close petal, purl 2 in front lps, open petal, purl 2 in front lps, close petal, purl 7 in front lps, seed border, turn. (*95 sts*)

Rows 34–36: Rep rows 26–28.

Row 37: Seed border, purl 10 in front lps, close petal, [purl 15 in front lps, close petal] twice, purl 10 in front lps, seed border, turn. *(83 sts)*

Row 38: Rep row 18.

Rows 39–104: [Rep rows 17–38 consecutively] 3 times.

Rows 105–111: Rep rows 17–23.

Rows 112–126: Rep rows 2–16. At end of last row, fasten off.

FINISHING

Cut 2 pieces of ribbon each 40 inches in length. Cut 2 pieces of ribbon each 50 inches in length.

Weave ribbon between seed border and body of Blankie working ribbon through every other st across top and bottom and through every other row on each side.

Tie ends in bows at corners and sew securely in place. Trim bow ends. ■

CABLES

One of the highlights of knitting are the beautiful intertwining cables one can create. When knitting and purling with a crochet hook, one can crochet those same exquisite cables in like fashion.

Unlike knitting where the loops have to remain on a needle or they unravel, in crochet, the loops wait patiently on the row. Therefore, although a cable needle *(a short, straight or slightly curved needle used to temporarily hold stitches)* or some form of holding device is mandatory to hold the loops when knitting cables, it is only highly recommended, for ease in doing the technique, when crocheting.

The basic stitches used to create the cable designs are the Reverse Stockinette stitch, used as a background on which to place the cables and the Stockinette Substitute stitch, used for the cables themselves. When working in rows from bottom to top, Reverse Stockinette naturally forms horizontal rows of bound-off stitches and Stockinette Sub creates vertical looking stitches needed to form columns of cables.

When working cable fabrics, stitches are formed in the front loop of stitches on right-side rows and are formed in the back loop of stitches on wrong-side rows. Therefore, all cable stitches, being worked on right-side rows, are worked in the front loop of the stitch.

Cable directions are written presuming one will be using a cable needle. However, for those who prefer not to use a cable needle, how to do the technique without a cable needle and how to do the technique using a second crochet hook in lieu of a cable needle will be explained later in this section.

Cable directions are written as follows:
Example: 2B/K3/PC

First, there is a number followed by the letter F or B. The number tells how many stitches to place on the cable needle and the letter tells whether to hold the stitches in the Front (F) of the work or in the Back (B) of the work.

Second, there is the letter K or P followed by a number. The letter indicates how one is to work the next few stitches on the row, either Knit (K) or Purl (P), and the number tells how many stitches are to be worked in that fashion.

Third, there is the letter K or P followed by the letter C. The first letter, K or P, tells one to Knit (K) or to Purl (P) the stitches on the Cable (C) needle.

Example: 2B/K3/PC means 2 Back, Knit 3, Purl Cable. Insert the cable needle purl wise through the front loop of each of the next two stitches and hold in Back of the work (2B), Knit the front loop of each of the next three stitches on the row (K3), Purl each stitch on the cable needle and slide it off the needle, working stitches on the cable needle in the same order they were placed on the needle, just as if they were still on the row (PC).

When placing stitches on a cable needle, always insert the needle purl wise through the front loop of the stitch closest to the hook first, then, when crocheting the stitches that are on the cable needle, start with the stitch that was placed on the needle first (stitches are picked up with one end of a cable needle, the stitches are slid down the needle to the other end and worked off so that the first stitch on is also the first stitch off).

ONE HOOK METHOD

If one doesn't wish to use a cable needle or 2nd crochet hook, work 2B/K3/PC as follows: Skip the next two stitches on the row *(the 2 in 2B)*, Knit the front loop of each of the next three stitches (K3), with hook in back of stitches just made *(the B in 2B)*, Purl the front loop of the first skipped stitch then Purl the front loop of the second skipped stitch (PC).

USING A SECOND CROCHET HOOK IN LIEU OF A CABLE NEEDLE METHOD

If one would like to use a 2nd crochet hook for a holding hook in lieu of using a cable needle, work 2B/K3/PC as follows:

Using holding hook, skip next stitch, insert holding hook knit wise through front loop of next stitch, then insert holding hook knit wise through front loop of skipped stitch *(two loops on hook).* Place holding hook in back of work, if desired—one can slide the loops into the head of the holding hook enabling the hook to dangle from the loops so that one doesn't have to hold onto the hook (2B). Knit the front loop of each of the next three stitches on the row (K3). Purl each loop on the holding hook and slide it off the hook, work stitches on the holding hook in the opposite order they were placed on the hook, just as if they were still on the row (PC).

If the directions were 3B/K3/PC, and one were using a holding hook, one would skip each of next two stitches on the row, insert hook knit wise through front loop of next stitch, then insert hook knit wise through front loop of second skipped stitch, then insert hook knit wise through front loop of first skipped stitch.

When using a 2nd crochet hook for a holding hook in lieu of a cable needle, always insert the hook knit wise through the front loop of the stitch that is the farthest away first, then, when crocheting the stitches that are on the holding hook, start with the stitch that was placed on the hook last (the stitch closest to the head of the hook).

FLARE
Cables tend to flare the fabric out at the beginning and at the end.

If one wishes to reduce the amount of flare at the beginning of one's work, divide the number of cable stitches that are to be crossed by two, then subtract that number from the number of stitches to be cast on. For example, if there are two cables with three stitches each that are going to be crossed, there are a total of six stitches. Divide the six stitches needed by two, giving an answer of three. On the first row, cast on three stitches for the cable instead of the needed six stitches. On the second row, add the subtracted stitches back in by working in the front loop and the back loop of the cable stitches that were cast on. For example, if one needs a six-stitch cable, CO/BO three stitches, then on the second row, work in the front loop and back loop of each of those three stitches so that there are a total of six stitches.

To reduce flare at the end of one's work: On the last row, decrease the cables the same number of stitches that were added on the second row.

One can also reduce flare by working the CO/BO row and the last row of the fabric with a smaller hook than will be used on the rest of the piece. This is a little less desirable than the first method because the tighter CO/BO row makes inserting the hook to create the second row a tight squeeze. But it works equally well. ∎

Coiled Rope Cable

Using the knit and purl with crochet hook method, one can crochet any cable pattern. Here are a few examples:

By twisting 2 sets of Stockinette Sub Stitches together on a Reverse Stockinette background, one can create a Coiled Rope Cable.

SPECIAL STITCHES

Cast On/Bind Off (CO/BO): See instructions and photos in Introduction on pages 6–8.

Knit: With yarn in back, insert hook from front to back in lp indicated, yo, pull through st and lp on hook.

Purl: With yarn in front, insert hook from back to front in lp indicated, yo, pull through st and lp on hook.

Knit 2 together (k2tog): Sk next st, insert hook knit wise through next st, then insert hook knit wise through sk st, yo, pull through both sts and lp on hook.

Cable: 3F/K3/KC, sl the front lp of each of next 3 sts on cable needle or 2nd crochet hook and hold in front of work (*3F*), knit in front lp of each of the next 3 sts on the row (*K3*), knit each st on cable needle or 2nd crochet hook and slide it off the needle or hook (*KC*).

INSTRUCTIONS

COILED ROPE

Row 1 (RS): Working from bottom to top, **CO/BO** (*see Special Stitches*) 6 sts for the cable plus number of sts desired for each side of cable for background, turn.

Row 2: Knit (*see Special Stitches*) in **back lps** (*see Stitch Guide*) across to 6 sts for cable, place marker, **purl** (*see Special Stitches*) 6 in back lps, place marker, knit in back lps across, turn.
Move markers each row.

Row 3: Purl in **front lps** (*see Stitch Guide*) across to first marker, knit 6 in front lps, purl in front lps across, turn.

Row 4: Rep row 2.

Row 5: Purl in front lps across to first marker, **cable** (*see Special Stitches*), purl in front lps across, turn.

Rep rows 2–5 consecutively for pattern.

TO REDUCE FLARE AT BEG

Work first 2 rows as follows:

Row 1: CO/BO 3 sts for cable plus the number of stitches desired for each side of cable for background, turn.

Row 2: Knit in back lps across to 3 sts for cable, place marker, (purl in front lp then purl in back lp) in each of next 3 sts (*3 st inc*), place marker, knit in back lps across, turn.

TO REDUCE FLARE AT END

Work pattern row 2, then work last row as follows:

Last row: Purl in front lps across to first marker, [k2tog (*see Special Stitches*) in front lps] 3 times (*3 st dec*), purl in front lps across. Fasten off. ∎

Braided Cable

One can create a braid by twisting three sets of Stockinette Sub stitches on a Reverse Stockinette background.

SPECIAL STITCHES

Cast On/Bind Off (CO/BO): See instructions and photos in Introduction on pages 6–8.

Knit: With yarn in back, insert hook from front to back in lp indicated, yo, pull through st and lp on hook.

Purl: With yarn in front, insert hook from back to front in lp indicated, yo, pull through st and lp on hook.

Knit 2 together (k2tog): Sk next st, insert hook knit wise through next st, then insert hook knit wise through sk st, yo, pull through both sts and lp on hook.

Cable A: 3B/K3/KC, sl the front lp of each of next 3 sts on cable needle or 2nd crochet hook and hold in back of work (3B), knit in front lp of each of the next 3 sts on the row (K3), knit each st on cable needle or 2nd crochet hook and slide it off the needle or hook (KC).

Cable B: 3F/K3/KC, sl the front lp of each of next 3 sts on cable needle or 2nd crochet hook and hold in front of work (3F), knit in front lp

of each of the next 3 sts on the row (K3), knit each st on cable needle or 2nd crochet hook and slide it off the needle or hook (KC).

INSTRUCTIONS

BRAIDED CABLE

Row 1 (RS): Working from bottom to top, **CO/ BO** (*see Special Stitches*) 9 sts for the cable plus number of sts desired for each side of cable for background, turn.

Row 2: Knit (*see Special Stitches*) in **back lps** (*see Stitch Guide*) across to 9 sts for cable, place marker, **purl** (*see Special Stitches*) 9 in back lps, place marker, knit in back lps across, turn.
Move markers each row.

Row 3: Purl in **front lps** (*see Stitch Guide*) across to first marker, knit 9 in front lps, purl in front lps across, turn.

Row 4: Rep row 2.

Row 5: Purl in front lps across to first marker, **cable A** (*see Special Stitches*), knit 3 in front lps, purl in front lps across, turn.

Row 6: Rep row 2.

Row 7: Purl in front lps across to first marker, knit 3 in front lps, **cable B** (*see Special Stitches*), purl in front lps across, turn.
Rep rows 4–7 consecutively for pattern.

TO REDUCE FLARE AT BEG

Work first 2 rows as follows:

Row 1: CO/BO 6 sts for cable plus the number of sts desired for each side of Cable for background, turn.

Row 2: Knit in back lps across to 6 sts for Cable, place marker, [(purl in front lp, purl in back lp) of next st, purl 1 in front lp] 3 times (*3 st inc*), place marker, knit in back lps across, turn.

TO REDUCE FLARE AT END

Work in pattern ending with row 4 or row 6, then work last row as follows:

Last row: Purl in front lps across to first marker, [**k2tog** (*see Special Stitches*) in front lps, knit 1 in front lp] 3 times (*3 st dec*), purl in front lps across. Fasten off. ∎

Chain Cable

If one separates two sets of Stockinette Sub Stitches, then brings them back together without twisting them, one can form a Chain Cable on a Reverse Stockinette background.

SPECIAL STITCHES

Cast On/Bind Off (CO/BO): See instructions and photos in Introduction on pages 6–8.

Knit: With yarn in back, insert hook from front to back in lp indicated, yo, pull through st and lp on hook.

Purl: With yarn in front, insert hook from back to front in lp indicated, yo, pull through st and lp on hook.

Knit 2 together (k2tog): Sk next st, insert hook knit wise through next st, then insert hook knit wise through sk st, yo, pull through both sts and lp on hook.

Cable A: 3B/K3/PC, sl the front lp of each of next 3 sts on cable needle or 2nd crochet hook and hold in back of work (3B), knit in front lp of each of the next 3 sts on the row (K3), purl each st on cable needle or 2nd crochet hook and slide it off the needle or hook (PC).

Cable B: 3F/P3/KC, sl the front lp of each of next 3 sts on cable needle or 2nd crochet hook and hold in front of work (3F), purl in front lp of each of the next 3 sts on the row (P3), knit each st on cable needle or 2nd crochet hook and slide it off the needle or hook (KC).

INSTRUCTIONS

CHAIN CABLE

Row 1 (RS): Working from bottom to top, **CO/ BO** (see Special Stitches) 12 sts for the cable plus number of sts desired for each side of cable for background, turn.

Row 2: Knit (see Special Stitches) in **back lps** (see Stitch Guide) across to 12 sts for cable, place maker, knit 3 in back lps, **purl** (see Special Stitches) 6 in back lps, knit 3 in back lps, place marker, knit in back lps across, turn.
Move markers each row.

Row 3: Purl in **front lps** (see Stitch Guide) across to first marker, purl 3 in front lps, knit 6 in front lps, purl 3 in front lps, purl in front lps across, turn.

Row 4: Rep row 2.

Row 5: Purl in front lps across to first marker, **cable A** (see Special Stitches), **cable B** (see Special Stitches), purl in front lps across, turn.

Row 6: Knit in back lps across to first marker, purl 3 in back lps, knit 6 in back lps, purl 3 in back lps, knit in back lps across, turn.

Row 7: Purl in front lps across to first marker, knit 3 in front lps, purl 6 in front lps, knit 3 in front lps, purl in front lps across, turn.

Row 8: Rep row 6.

Row 9: Purl in front lps across to first marker, cable B, cable A, purl in front lps across, turn.
Rep rows 2–9 consecutively for pattern.

TO REDUCE FLARE AT BEG

Work first 2 rows as follows:

Row 1: CO/BO 9 sts for cable plus number of sts desired for each side of cable for background, turn.

Row 2: Knit in back lps across to 9 sts for cable, place marker, knit 3 in back lps, (purl in front lp, purl in back lp) of each of next 3 sts (3 st inc), knit 3 in back lps, place marker, knit in back lps across, turn.

TO REDUCE FLARE AT END

Work in pattern ending with row 2, then work last row as follows:

Last row: Purl in front lps across to first marker, purl 3 in front lps, [**k2tog** (see Special Stitches) in front lps] 3 times (3 st dec), purl 3 in front lps, purl in front lps across. Fasten off. ∎

Maverick Cable

By separating sets of Stockinette Sub Stitch, and then not bringing them back together, one can form a Maverick Cable on a Reverse Stockinette background.

SPECIAL STITCHES

Cast On/Bind Off (CO/BO): See instructions and photos in Introduction on pages 6–8.

Knit: With yarn in back, insert hook from front to back in lp indicated, yo, pull through st and lp on hook.

Purl: With yarn in front, insert hook from back to front in lp indicated, yo, pull through st and lp on hook.

Knit 2 together (k2tog): Sk next st, insert hook knit wise through next st, then insert hook knit wise through sk st, yo, pull through both sts and lp on hook.

Cable A: 3B/K3/KC, sl the front lp of each of next 3 sts on cable needle or 2nd crochet hook and hold in back of work (3B), knit in front lp of each of the next 3 sts on the row (K3), knit each st on cable needle or 2nd crochet hook and slide it off the needle or hook (KC).

Cable B: 3F/K3/KC, sl the front lp of each of next 3 sts on cable needle or 2nd crochet hook and hold in front of work (3F), knit in front lp of each of the next 3 sts on the row (K3), knit each st on cable needle or 2nd crochet hook and slide it off the needle or hook (KC).

INSTRUCTIONS

MAVERICK CABLE

Row 1 (RS): Working from bottom to top, **CO/BO** (*see Special Stitches*) 12 sts for the cable plus number of sts desired for each side of cable for background, turn.

Row 2: Knit (*see Special Stitches*) in **back lps** (*see Stitch Guide*) across to 12 sts for cable, place marker, **purl** (*see Special Stitches*) 12 in back lps, place marker, knit in back lps across, turn.

Move markers each row.

Row 3: Purl in **front lps** (*see Stitch Guide*) across to first marker, knit 12 in front lps, purl in front lps across, turn.

Row 4: Rep row 2.

Row 5: Purl in front lps across to first marker, **cable A** (*see Special Stitches*), **cable B** (*see Special Stitches*), purl in front lps across, turn.

Rep rows 2–5 for pattern.

TO REDUCE FLARE AT BEG

Work first 2 rows as follows:

Row 1: CO/BO 6 sts for cable plus the number of sts desired for each side of cable for background, turn.

Row 2: Knit in back lps across to 6 sts for cable, place marker, (purl in front lp, purl in back lp) of each of next 6 sts (*6 st inc*), place marker, knit in back lps across, turn.

TO REDUCE FLARE AT END

Work in pattern ending with row 2, then work last row as follows:

Last row: Purl in front lps across to first marker, [**k2tog** (*see Special Stitches*) in front lps] 6 times (*6 st dec*), purl in front lps across. Fasten off. ∎

Diagonal Cable

One can also move sets of Stockinette Sub stitches across a Reverse Stockinette background in a diagonal path so that the sets never cross creating an all-over pattern.

SPECIAL STITCHES

Cast On/Bind Off (CO/BO): See instructions and photos in Introduction on pages 6–8.

Knit: With yarn in back, insert hook from front to back in lp indicated, yo, pull through st and lp on hook.

Purl: With yarn in front, insert hook from back to front in lp indicated, yo, pull through st and lp on hook.

Cable: 2F/P2/KC, sl the front lp of each of next 2 sts on cable needle or 2nd crochet hook and hold in front of work (2F), purl in front lp of each of the next 2 sts on the row (P2), knit each st on cable needle or 2nd crochet hook and slide it off the needle or hook (KC).

INSTRUCTIONS

DIAGONAL CABLE

Row 1 (RS): Working from bottom to top, **CO/BO** (*see Special Stitches*) a multiple of 6 sts plus 2, turn.

Row 2: Purl (*see Special Stitches*) 2 in **back lps** (*see Stitch Guide*), [**knit** (*see Special Stitches*) 4 in back lps, purl 2 in back lps] across, turn.

Row 3: [**Cable** (*see Special Stitches*), purl 2 in **front lps** (*see Stitch Guide*)] across to last 2 sts, purl last 2 sts in front lps, turn.

Row 4: Knit 2 in back lps, [knit 2 in back lps, purl 2 in back lps, knit 2 in back lps] across, turn.

Row 5: Purl 2 in front lps, [cable, purl 2 in front lps] across, turn.

Row 6: Knit 2 in back lps, [purl 2 in back lps, knit 4 in back lps] across, turn.

Row 7: Knit 2 in front lps, [purl 2 in front lps, cable] across, turn.

Rep rows 2–7 consecutively for pattern. ∎

Honeycomb Cable

By omitting the Reverse Stockinette stitches one can create an all-over design using the Stockinette Sub stitch for both the cables and the background.

SPECIAL STITCHES

Cast On/Bind Off (CO/BO): See instructions and photos in Introduction on pages 6–8.

Knit: With yarn in back, insert hook from front to back in lp indicated, yo, pull through st and lp on hook.

Purl: With yarn in front, insert hook from back to front in lp indicated, yo, pull through st and lp on hook.

Knit 2 together (k2tog): Sk next st, insert hook knit wise through next st, then insert hook knit wise through sk st, yo, pull through both sts and lp on hook.

Cable A: 2B/K2/KC, sl the front lp of each of next 2 sts on cable needle or 2nd crochet hook and hold in back of work (2B), knit in front lp of each of the next 2 sts on the row (K2), knit each st on cable needle or 2nd crochet hook and slide it off the needle or hook (KC).

Cable B: 2F/K2/KC, sl the front lp of each of next 2 sts on cable needle or 2nd crochet hook and hold in front of work (2F), knit in front lp of each of the next 2 sts on the row (K2), knit each st on cable needle or 2nd crochet hook and slide it off the needle or hook (KC).

INSTRUCTIONS

HONEYCOMB CABLE

Row 1 (RS): Working from bottom to top, **CO/ BO** *(see Special Stitches)* in a multiple of 8 sts, turn.

Row 2: Purl *(see Special Stitches)* in **back lps** *(see Stitch Guide)* across, turn.

Row 3: Knit *(see Special Stitches)* in **front lps** *(see Stitch Guide)* across, turn.

Row 4: Rep row 2.

Row 5: [**Cable A** *(see Special Stitches)*, **cable B** *(see Special Stitches)*] across, turn.

Rows 6 & 7: Rep rows 2 and 3.

Row 8: Rep row 2.

Row 9: [Cable B, cable A] across, turn.

Rep rows 2–9 consecutively for pattern.

TO REDUCE FLARE AT BEG

Work first 2 rows as follows:

Row 1: CO/BO in a multiple of 4 sts, turn.

Row 2: (Purl in front lp, purl in back lp) of each st across, turn.

TO REDUCE FLARE AT END

Work in pattern ending with row 2 or row 6, then work last row as follows:

Last row: K2tog *(see Special Stitches)* in front lps across. Fasten off. ■

Casual Cable Throw

SKILL LEVEL

INTERMEDIATE

FINISHED SIZE
44 x 52 inches

MATERIALS
- Patons SWS medium (worsted) weight yarn (2¾ oz/110 yds/80g per skein):
  17 skeins #70530 natural geranium
- Sizes L/11/8mm and M/13/9mm crochet hooks or size needed to obtain gauge
- Cable needle or 2nd crochet hook

GAUGE
Size M hook: 15 sts = 4 inches; 14 rows = 4 inches

PATTERN NOTE
Size L hook is used to work first 2 rows of Throw and last 2 rows to help control cable flare.

SPECIAL STITCHES
Cast On/Bind Off (CO/BO): See instructions and photos in Introduction on pages 6–8.

Knit: With yarn in back, insert hook from front to back in lp indicated, yo, pull through st and lp on hook.

Purl: With yarn in front, insert hook from back to front in lp indicated, yo, pull through st and lp on hook.

Cable A: 3F/P1/KC, sl the front lp of each of next 3 sts on cable needle or 2nd crochet hook and hold in front of work (3F), purl in front lp of next st on the row (P1), knit each st on cable needle or 2nd crochet hook and slide it off the needle or hook (KC).

Cable B: 1B/K3/PC, sl the front lp of next st on cable needle or 2nd crochet hook and hold in back of work (1B), knit in front lp of each of the next 3 sts on the row (K3), purl each st on cable needle or 2nd crochet hook and slide it off the needle or hook (PC).

Cable C: 3F/K3/KC, sl the front lp of each of next 3 sts on cable needle or 2nd crochet hook and hold in front of work (3F), knit in front lp of each of next 3 sts on the row (K3), knit each st on cable needle or 2nd crochet hook and slide it off the needle or hook (KC).

INSTRUCTIONS

THROW
Row 1 (RS): With **size L hook** (*see Pattern Note*), **CO/BO** (*see Special Stitches*) 165 sts, turn.

Row 2: Purl (*see Special Stitches*) 3 in **back lps** (*see Stitch Guide*), [**knit** (*see Special Stitches*) 6 in back lps, purl 3 in back lps] across, turn.

Row 3: With size M hook, knit 3 in **front lps** (*see Stitch Guide*), [purl 6 in front lps, knit 3 in front lps] across, turn.

Row 4: Rep row 2.

Row 5: Knit 3 in front lps, [purl 6 in front lps, **cable A** (*see Special Stitches*), purl 4 in front lps, **cable B** (*see Special Stitches*), purl 6 in front lps, knit 3 in front lps] across, turn.

Row 6: Purl 3 in back lps, [knit 7 in back lps, purl 3 in back lps, knit 4 in back lps, purl 3 in back lps, knit 7 in back lps, purl 3 in back lps] across, turn.

Row 7: Knit 3 in front lps, [purl 7 in front lps, cable A, purl 2 in front lps, cable B, purl 7 in front lps, knit 3 in front lps] across, turn.

Row 8: Purl 3 in back lps, [knit 8 in back lps, purl 3 in back lps, knit 2 in back lps, purl 3 in back lps, knit 8 in back lps, purl 3 in back lps] across, turn.

Row 9: Knit 3 in front lps, [purl 8 in front lps, cable A, cable B, purl 8 in front lps, knit 3 in front lps] across, turn.

Row 10: Purl 3 in back lps, [knit 9 in back lps, purl 6 in back lps, knit 9 in back lps, purl 3 in back lps] across, turn.

Row 11: Knit 3 in front lps, [purl 9 in front lps, **cable C** (*see Special Stitches*), purl 9 in front lps, knit 3 in front lps] across, turn.

Row 12: Rep row 10.

Row 13: Knit 3 in front lps, [purl 8 in front lps, cable B, cable A, purl 8 in front lps, knit 3 in front lps] across, turn.

Row 14: Rep row 8.

Row 15: Knit 3 in front lps, [purl 7 in front lps, cable B, purl 2 in front lps, cable A, purl 7 in front lps, knit 3 in front lps] across, turn.

Row 16: Rep row 6.

Row 17: Knit 3 in front lps, [purl 6 in front lps, cable B, purl 4 in front lps, cable A, purl 6 in front lps, knit 3 in front lps] across, turn.

Rows 18 & 19: Rep rows 2 and 3.

Rows 20–181: [Rep rows 2–19 consecutively] 9 times.

Row 182: With size L hook, rep row 2.

Row 183: Purl in front lps across. Fasten off. ∎

Reverse Stockinette Cable Sweater

SKILL LEVEL

INTERMEDIATE

FINISHED SIZES

Instructions given fit child's size 4 (*small*); changes for size 6 (*medium*), size 8 (*large*) and size 10 (*X-large*) are in [ ].

FINISHED GARMENT MEASUREMENTS

Chest: 27 inches (*small*) [29 inches (*medium*), 30½ inches (*large*), 32 inches (*X-large*)]

MATERIALS

- Red Heart Classic medium (worsted) weight yarn (3½ oz/190 yds/99g per skein): 3 [4, 5, 5] skeins #615 artichoke
- Size L/11/8mm crochet hook or size needed to obtain gauge
- Cable needle or 2nd crochet hook
- Tapestry needle

MEDIUM

GAUGE

12 sts = 4 inches; 16 rows = 4 inches
Take time to check gauge.

PATTERN NOTE

Join with slip stitch as indicated unless otherwise stated.

SPECIAL STITCHES

Cast On/Bind Off (CO/BO): See instructions and photos in Introduction on pages 6–8.
Knit: With yarn in back, insert hook from front to back in lp indicated, yo, pull through st and lp on hook.
Purl: With yarn in front, insert hook from back to front in lp indicated, yo, pull through st and lp on hook.
Cable: 3F/K3/KC, sl the front lp of each of next 3 sts on cable needle or 2nd crochet hook and hold in front of work (3F), knit in front lp of each of the next 3 sts on the row (K3), knit each st on cable needle or 2nd crochet hook and slide it off the needle or hook (KC).
Knit 2 together (k2tog): Sk next st, insert hook knit wise through next st, then insert hook knit wise through sk st, yo, pull through both sts and lp on hook.

INSTRUCTIONS

SWEATER

BACK RIBBING
Row 1: CO/BO (*see Special Stitches*) 5 sts, turn.
Rows 2–46 [2–50, 2–53, 2–55]: Knit (*see Special Stitches*) in **back lps** (*see Stitch Guide*) across, turn.

BACK
Row 1 (RS): Working in ends of rows on Back Ribbing, evenly sp 40 [44, 47, 49] knit sts across, turn.
Row 2: Knit in back lps across, turn.
Row 3: Purl (*see Special Stitches*) in **front lps** (*see Stitch Guide*) across, turn.
Next rows: Rep rows 2 and 3 for pattern until piece measures 9½ [10, 11¾, 13] inches from beg.

ARMHOLE SHAPING
Row 1: Work in pattern across, leaving last 3 [4, 4, 4] sts unworked, turn. (*37 [40, 43, 45] sts*)
Row 2: Rep row 1. (*34 [36, 39, 41] sts*)
Next rows: Continue working in pattern and at same time, dec 1 st at end of every row 6 [6, 8, 8] times. (*28 [30, 31, 33] sts at end of last row*)
Next rows: Work even in pattern until piece measures 5 [5½, 5¾, 6] inches from beg of Armhole Shaping, ending with RS row.

FIRST SHOULDER SHAPING
Row 1 (WS): Work in pattern across first 7 [8, 8, 9] sts leaving rem sts unworked, turn.
Row 2: Work in pattern across. Fasten off.

2ND SHOULDER SHAPING
Row 1: Sk next 14 [14, 15, 15] sts, **join** (*see Pattern Note*) in next st, work in pattern across, turn. (*7 [8, 8, 9] sts*)
Row 2: Work in pattern across. Fasten off.

FRONT RIBBING
Work same as Back Ribbing.

FRONT
Row 1 (RS): Working in ends of rows on Front Ribbing, evenly sp 46 [50, 53, 55] knit sts across, turn.
Row 2: Knit 9 [10, 11, 12] in back lps, purl 6 in back lps, knit 16 [18, 19, 19] in back lps, purl 6

in back lps, knit 9 [10, 11, 12] in back lps, turn.

Row 3: Purl 9 [10, 11, 12] in front lps, knit 6 in front lps, purl 16 [18, 19, 19] in front lps, knit 6 in front lps, purl 9 [10, 11, 12] in front lps, turn.

Row 4: Rep row 2.

Row 5: Purl 9 [10, 11, 12] in front lps, **cable** (*see Special Stitches*), purl 16 [18, 19, 19] in front lps, cable, purl 9 [10, 11, 12] in front lps, turn.

Rows 6 & 7: Rep rows 2 and 3.

Rows 8–11: Rep rows 2–5.

Next rows: Rep rows 6–11 consecutively for pattern until piece measures 9½ [10, 11¾, 13] inches from beg.

ARMHOLE SHAPING

Row 1: Work in pattern across, leaving last 3 [4, 4, 4] sts unworked, turn. (*43 [46, 49, 51] sts*)

Row 2: Rep row 1. (*40 [42, 45, 47] sts*)

Next rows: Continue working in pattern and at same time, dec 1 st at end of every row 6 [6, 8, 8] times. (*34 [36, 37, 39] sts at end of last row*)

Next rows: Work even in pattern until Front has 6 [6, 8, 8] rows less than the back.

FIRST NECK SHAPING

Row 1: Work in pattern across first 14 [15, 15, 16] sts, leaving rem sts unworked, turn.

Next rows: Work in pattern and **at the same time** dec 1 st at neck edge every row 4 times. (*10 [11, 11, 12] sts at end of last row*)

Next rows: Work even in pattern until piece is 1 row less than Back.

Last row (RS): Purl 1 [2, 2, 2] in front lps, [**k2tog** (*see Special Stitches*) in front lps] 3 times, purl 3 [3, 3, 4] in front lps. Fasten off. (*7 [8, 8, 9] sts*)

2ND NECK SHAPING

Row 1: Sk next 6 [6, 7, 7] sts, join in next st, work in pattern across, turn. (*14 [15, 15, 16] sts*)

Next rows: Work in pattern and **at the same time** dec 1 st at neck edge every row 4 times. (*10 [11, 11, 12] sts at end of last row*)

Next rows: Work even in pattern until piece is 1 row less than Back.

Last row (RS): Purl 3 [3, 3, 4] in front lps, [k2tog in front lps] 3 times, purl 1 [2, 2, 2] in front lps. Fasten off. (*7 [8, 8, 9] sts*)

SLEEVE
MAKE 2.

RIBBING

Row 1: CO/BO 5 sts, turn.

Rows 2–24 [2–24, 2–26, 2–26]: Knit in back lps across, turn.

BODY

Row 1 (RS): Working in ends of rows on Sleeve Ribbing, evenly sp 24 [24, 26, 26] knit sts across, turn.

Row 2: Knit in back lps across, turn.

Row 3: Purl in front lps across, turn.

Next rows: Rep rows 2 and 3 alternately for pattern and at the same time inc 1 st at end of next row, then inc 1 st at end of every 5th [3rd, 3rd, 3rd] row 5 [7, 7, 9] times. (*30 [32, 34, 36] sts at end of last row*)

Next rows: Work even in pattern until piece measures 10½ [11½, 12½, 14] inches from beg.

SLEEVE CAP

Row 1: Work in pattern across leaving last 3 [4, 4, 4] sts unworked, turn. (*27 [28, 30, 32] sts*)

Row 2: Rep row 1. (*24 [24, 26, 28] sts*)

Next rows: Work in pattern and **at same time dec** 1 st at end of every row 4 [2, 2, 2] times. (*20 [22, 24, 26] sts at end of last row*)

Next rows: Work even in pattern until piece measures 3 inches from beg of Sleeve Cap.

Next row: Work in pattern across leaving last 3 sts unworked, turn. (*17 [19, 21, 23] sts*)

Next rows: Rep last row until there are 8 [10, 12, 14] sts rem. At end of last row, fasten off.

ASSEMBLY

Sew shoulder seams.

Fold 1 Sleeve in half lengthwise, place fold at shoulder seam, sew in place.

Rep with rem Sleeve.

Sew Sleeve and side seams.

NECK EDGING

With RS facing, join at neck edge, evenly sp an even number of knit st around, join in front lp of beg st, turn.

NECK RIBBING

Row 1 (WS): Ch 3, knit in back of each ch, knit in back lp of first 2 sts on Neck Edging, leaving rem sts unworked, turn.

Row 2: Sk first 2 knit sts on Neck Edging, knit 3 in back lps, turn.

Row 3: Knit 3 in back lps, knit in back lps of next 2 sts on Neck Edging, turn.

Next rows: Rep row 2 and 3 alternately for pattern around Neck Edging, ending with row 2. At end of last row, fasten off.

Sew first and last rows tog. ■

Stitch Guide

For more complete information, visit **FreePatterns.com**

ABBREVIATIONS

beg	begin/begins/beginning
bpdc	back post double crochet
bpsc	back post single crochet
bptr	back post treble crochet
CC	contrasting color
ch(s)	chain(s)
ch-	refers to chain or space previously made (e.g., ch-1 space)
ch sp(s)	chain space(s)
cl(s)	cluster(s)
cm	centimeter(s)
dc	double crochet (singular/plural)
dc dec	double crochet 2 or more stitches together, as indicated
dec	decrease/decreases/decreasing
dtr	double treble crochet
ext	extended
fpdc	front post double crochet
fpsc	front post single crochet
fptr	front post treble crochet
g	gram(s)
hdc	half double crochet
hdc dec	half double crochet 2 or more stitches together, as indicated
inc	increase/increases/increasing
lp(s)	loop(s)
MC	main color
mm	millimeter(s)
oz	ounce(s)
pc	popcorn(s)
rem	remain/remains/remaining
rep(s)	repeat(s)
rnd(s)	round(s)
RS	right side
sc	single crochet (singular/plural)
sc dec	single crochet 2 or more stitches together, as indicated
sk	skip/skipped/skipping
sl st(s)	slip stitch(es)
sp(s)	space(s)/spaced
st(s)	stitch(es)
tog	together
tr	treble crochet
trtr	triple treble
WS	wrong side
yd(s)	yard(s)
yo	yarn over

Chain—ch: Yo, pull through lp on hook.

Slip stitch—sl st: Insert hook in st, pull through both lps on hook.

Single crochet—sc: Insert hook in st, yo, pull through st, yo, pull through both lps on hook.

Front post stitch—fp: Back post stitch—bp: When working post st, insert hook from right to left around post st on previous row.

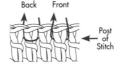

Front loop—front lp Back loop—back lp

Front Loop   Back Loop

Half double crochet—hdc: Yo, insert hook in st, yo, pull through st, yo, pull through all 3 lps on hook.

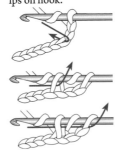

Double crochet—dc: Yo, insert hook in st, yo, pull through st, [yo, pull through 2 lps] twice.

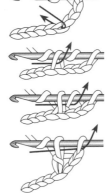

Change colors: Drop first color; with 2nd color, pull through last 2 lps of st.

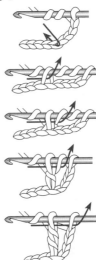

Treble crochet—tr: Yo twice, insert hook in st, yo, pull through st, [yo, pull through 2 lps] 3 times.

Double treble crochet—dtr: Yo 3 times, insert hook in st, yo, pull through st, [yo, pull through 2 lps] 4 times.

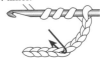

Single crochet decrease (sc dec): (Insert hook, yo, draw lp through) in each of the sts indicated, yo, draw through all lps on hook.

Example of 2-sc dec

Half double crochet decrease (hdc dec): (Yo, insert hook, yo, draw lp through) in each of the sts indicated, yo, draw through all lps on hook.

Example of 2-hdc dec

Double crochet decrease (dc dec): (Yo, insert hook, yo, draw loop through, draw through 2 lps on hook) in each of the sts indicated, yo, draw through all lps on hook.

Example of 2-dc dec

Example of 2-tr dec

Treble crochet decrease (tr dec): Holding back last lp of each st, tr in each of the sts indicated, yo, pull through all lps on hook.

US		UK
sl st (slip stitch)	=	sc (single crochet)
sc (single crochet)	=	dc (double crochet)
hdc (half double crochet)	=	htr (half treble crochet)
dc (double crochet)	=	tr (treble crochet)
tr (treble crochet)	=	dtr (double treble crochet)
dtr (double treble crochet)	=	ttr (triple treble crochet)
skip	=	miss

Metric conversion charts

INCHES INTO MILLIMETRES & CENTIMETRES (Rounded off slightly)

inches	mm	cm	inches	cm	inches	cm	inches	cm
1/8	3	0.3	5	12.5	21	53.5	38	96.5
1/4	6	0.6	5 1/2	14	22	56	39	99
3/8	10	1	6	15	23	58.5	40	101.5
1/2	13	1.3	7	18	24	61	41	104
5/8	15	1.5	8	20.5	25	63.5	42	106.5
3/4	20	2	9	23	26	66	43	109
7/8	22	2.2	10	25.5	27	68.5	44	112
1	25	2.5	11	28	28	71	45	114.5
1 1/4	32	3.2	12	30.5	29	73.5	46	117
1 1/2	38	3.8	13	33	30	76	47	119.5
1 3/4	45	4.5	14	35.5	31	79	48	122
2	50	5	15	38	32	81.5	49	124.5
2 1/2	65	6.5	16	40.5	33	84	50	127
3	75	7.5	17	43	34	86.5		
3 1/2	90	9	18	46	35	89		
4	100	10	19	48.5	36	91.5		
4 1/2	115	11.5	20	51	37	94		

KNITTING NEEDLES CONVERSION CHART

Canada/U.S.	0	1	2	3	4	5	6	7	8	9	10	10½	11	13	15
Metric (mm)	2	2¼	2¾	3¼	3½	3¾	4	4½	5	5½	6	6½	8	9	10

CROCHET HOOKS CONVERSION CHART

Canada/U.S.	1/B	2/C	3/D	4/E	5/F	6/G	8/H	9/I	10/J	10½/K	N
Metric (mm)	2.25	2.75	3.25	3.5	3.75	4.25	5	5.5	6	6.5	9.0

METRIC CONVERSIONS

yards	x	.9144	=	metres (m)
yards	x	91.44	=	centimetres (cm)
inches	x	2.54	=	centimetres (cm)
inches	x	25.40	=	millimetres (mm)
inches	x	.0254	=	metres (m)

centimetres	x	.3937	=	inches
metres	x	1.0936	=	yards

Knit 1, Purl 2 in Crochet is published by DRG, 306 East Parr Road, Berne, IN 46711. Printed in USA.
Copyright © 2009 DRG. All rights reserved. This publication may not be reproduced
in part or in whole without written permission from the publisher.

RETAIL STORES: If you would like to carry this pattern book or any other DRG publications, visit DRGwholesale.com.

Every effort has been made to ensure that the instructions in this publication are complete and accurate.
We cannot, however, take responsibility for human error, typographical mistakes or variations in individual work.
Please visit AnniesCustomerCare.com to check for pattern updates.

ISBN: 978-1-59635-286-5   3 4 5 6 7 8 9

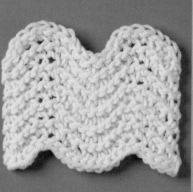

knit 1 purl 2 *in Crochet*

Known for her unique Learn To style books, designer Bendy Carter has done it again. All of the designs in *Knit 1, Purl 2 in Crochet* are created using two stitches, the Knit Stitch and the Purl Stitch. Although the stitches are worked with a crochet hook, they are worked in a similar fashion as if using knitting needles.

To work a knit stitch, o[...] in the back of the work, then inserts the [...] e knitting needle through the stitch (on[...] e front of the work to the back of the wor[...] around the crochet hook or the knitting ne[...] hrough the stitch.

To work a purl stitch, o[...] n the front of the work then, inserts the c[...] knitting needle through a stitch (one lo[...] ck of the work to the front of the work, [...] ound the crochet hook or the knitting nee[...] ough the stitch.

Using a crochet hook, i[...] g needle, creates only one extra step. When using a crochet hook, the wrapped yarn that is pulled through the stitch must also be pulled through the loop on the hook. In knitting, this is known as binding off. By combining knit and purl stitches within a given work, one can crochet beautiful fabric including cables, ribbing, bobbles and a variety of texture stitches.

You will find over 40 stitches including stockinette, cable, bobble, texture and lace, and 12 projects, plus step-by-step instructions and color photographs.

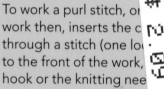

U.S. $14.95 CANADA $17.95

UPC

7 32526 40430 6

PRINTED IN USA
AnniesAttic.com

EAN
ISBN: 978-1-59635-286-5

5 14 9

9 781596 352865

CREATING GOURD BIRDS

with the *Fairy Gourdmother*®

Schiffer

Sammie Crawford

Sammie Crawford, a professional designer, author, and teacher, has been painting since 1987 and has published five books on gourd painting. She has taught at many national venues including Society of Decorative Painters convention, Tole Country and is a regular at the Gourd Gathering in Cherokee, North Carolina, where she teaches her love of gourd painting. She enjoys the challenges of painting and designing on the three-dimensional surfaces that gourds offer.

National television appearances and travel-teaching have allowed her to lecture and demonstrate the versatility of gourds and spread her "gourd gospel." Among her proudest accomplishments are having her artwork on the Christmas trees of the Smithsonian and the Library of Congress and on the White House tree three times.

Sammie belongs to two wonderful organizations that "have benefited me greatly": The Society of Decorative Painters, 393 McLean Blvd., Wichita, KS, 67203-5868, and The American Gourd Society, 317 Maple Court, Kokomo, IN, 46902-3633. Says Sammie, "They keep me in touch with like-minded people and new developments in the gourd and art worlds." She encourages other artists to join these organizations.

To contact Sammie, write her at

170 Russey Road, Hot Springs, AR 71913-9781, or call her at 501-525-8558. Her e-mail address is gourdfairy@aol.com and her website is **TheFairyGourdmother.com.**